STAY OF EXECUTION

THE HOOVER
INSTITUTION

HOOVER STUDIES IN POLITICS, ECONOMICS, AND SOCIETY

General Editors
Peter Berkowitz and Tod Lindberg

OTHER TITLES IN THE SERIES

STAY OF EXECUTION

Saving the Death Penalty from Itself

Charles Lane

HOOVER STUDIES IN POLITICS, ECONOMICS, AND SOCIETY

Published in cooperation with
HOOVER INSTITUTION
Stanford University • Stanford, California

ROWMAN & LITTLEFIELD PUBLISHERS, INC.
Lanham • Boulder • New York • Toronto • Plymouth, UK

ROWMAN & LITTLEFIELD PUBLISHERS, INC.

www.hoover.org

Published in the United States of America by Rowman & Littlefield Publishers, Inc.
A wholly owned subsidiary of The Rowman & Littlefield Publishing Group, Inc.
4501 Forbes Boulevard, Suite 200, Lanham, Maryland 20706
www.rowmanlittlefield.com
Estover Road
Plymouth PL6 7PY
United Kingdom
Distributed by National Book Network

First printing, 2010
16 15 14 13 12 11 10 09   9 8 7 6 5 4 3 2 1
Manufactured in the United States of America

British Library Cataloguing in Publication Information Available

Library of Congress Cataloging-in-Publication Data

Lane, Charles, 1961–
   Stay of execution : saving the death penalty from itself / Charles Lane.
     p. cm. — (Hoover studies in politics, economics, and society)
   Includes bibliographical references and index.
   ISBN 978-1-4422-0378-5 (cloth : alk. paper) — ISBN 978-1-4422-0380-8
(electronic : alk. paper)
   1. Capital punishment—United States. 2. Capital punishment—Moral and ethical
aspects—United States. I. Title.
HV8699.U5L366 2010
364.660973—dc22   2010027068

♾™ The paper used in this publication meets the minimum requirements of American National Standard for Information Sciences—Permanence of Paper for Printed Library Materials, ANSI/NISO Z39.48-1992.

For my parents

CONTENTS

PREFACE

There was an unmistakable tone of resignation in the words coming through the telephone. The voice belonged to a senior Texas official, a man with significant experience in, and responsibility for, making sure the death penalty is carried out in his state, which executes more convicted criminals than any other U.S. jurisdiction. He enjoyed his work and thought it necessary. In his view, capital punishment was, and should be, one weapon in society's crime-fighting arsenal. But lately, he confided, he had begun to doubt that it would exist much longer—even in Texas. "The death penalty's probably got ten or twenty years left in it," he told me. "It's never going to go away, but it'll probably stop being used."[1]

It was a remarkable forecast, considering not only its source, but also the wider social and historical context. The death penalty has been a part of American law and culture since British colonists stepped ashore in Virginia more than 400 years ago. Used as a punishment for all sorts of crimes before the American Revolution—including petty offenses, or invented ones, like witchcraft—execution was clearly, if implicitly, authorized in the Constitution and continued, albeit under varying circumstances, throughout the nineteenth and twentieth centuries. All told, 15,627 people were executed under civil and military authority in the U.S. from 1608 through 2008; of these, 1,136 were put to death between the start of the "modern" phase of capital punishment in 1977 and the end of 2008.[2]

Today, polls show that the vast majority of Americans still believe that murderers should be put to death, at least in theory. And although the states do not unanimously permit capital punishment—35 states have a death penalty while 15 states plus the District of Co-

lumbia do not—it is still the law of the land in
the entire United States, in the sense that federal law prescribes death for certain crimes, as
does the armed forces' Uniform Code of Military Justice. Under existing Supreme Court
precedent, the death penalty is plainly constitutional. The comments, both official and un-
official, of the nine members of the current
court suggest that none of them—not even
those who have been harshly critical of capital
punishment's implementation—would vote to
abolish it. Over the last three-plus decades,
the U.S. retained the death penalty even as
other democracies in the English-speaking
world and continental Europe got rid of it.

Nevertheless, as the Texas official well understood, in recent years the U.S. death
penalty has gone into a noticeable decline. The
list of 35 death penalty states is 3 shorter than
it was 5 years ago. During that time, two pop-
ulous states, New York and New Jersey, and
one small one, New Mexico, have abolished
capital punishment, and other states came
close to doing so. Meanwhile, an effort supported by then-Governor Mitt Romney to reinstate the death penalty in Massachusetts
failed. Death sentences have been decreasing
fairly steadily since 1996, when they reached
a post-1977 peak of 317. In 2008, courts is-

sued just 111 death sentences—a 30-year low. As of the end of that year, the U.S. death sentence rate was the same as it had been three decades earlier—roughly seven death sentences for every 1,000 murders—and the rate appeared to be dropping still.

*Death Sentences per 1000 Murders
1977-2008*

Source: Author calculations based on FBI Uniform Crime Reports and U.S. Department of Justice, Bureau of Justice Statistics, "Capital Punishment Statistics."

Death row grew from 1977 to 2000, when its population reached nearly 3,600, but has since begun to shrink, to approximately 3,200 inmates by the beginning of 2008.[3]

Death Row's Population
1977-2007

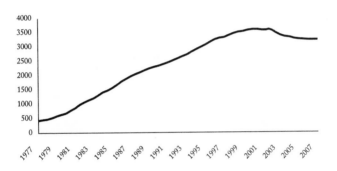

Source: U.S. Department of Justice, Bureau of Justice Statistics, "Capital Punishment Statistics," Prisoners on Death Row, 1953–2007.

Death row is not getting smaller because its inmates are being put to death more frequently. To the contrary, fewer and fewer death sentences are actually being carried out. The annual number of executions hit its post-1977 peak of 98 in 1999. Over the following decade, the rate steadily declined until, in 2008, there were just 37 executions—a decrease of more than 62 percent from the 1999 record.[4]

Executions 1977-2008

Source: U.S. Department of Justice, Bureau of Justice Statistics, "Capital Punishment Statistics," Executions, 1930-2008.

This is a book about the causes and implications of this trend. I argue that the death penalty's decline does not reflect any growing public disenchantment with capital punishment, as many in the media and academia have argued. Rather, it has more to do with the unanticipated consequence of another broad—and salutary—trend in contemporary American life: the steep nationwide decline in violent crime. Quite simply, fewer murders means fewer occasions for states to seek or impose capital punishment. To be sure, less crime makes the public feel more secure, and may therefore reduce the overt political demand for capital punishment. However, as I also show, overwhelming survey evidence shows that the public's support for capital punishment remains strong.

I both recognize the political power of the pro-death penalty American majority and share its moral judgment. Accordingly, I argue that the death penalty's disappearance in the U.S. is neither inevitable nor desirable. However, unlike some supporters of capital punishment, I also recognize that, as the death penalty has declined, troubling flaws in its implementation have stood out more starkly. In my view, though, these are not necessarily the ones most frequently cited by judges, politicians, or the media: alleged racial bias and the risk of executing innocent people. Rather, the most intractable issue is the lack of consistent standards for the imposition of the death penalty, such that various jurisdictions may use it, or not, according to no clear moral logic.

The decline of the death penalty creates an opportunity to remedy that problem and to do so in a way that would probably also ameliorate lingering concerns over race and innocence. The goal of reform should be a death penalty that is more consistently and more specifically targeted than the version we have now. It would focus on those who commit the most monstrous and socially destabilizing crimes—and who pose a clear danger of doing so again. And, contrary to partisans on both sides of the debate, I believe such a radical reform is not only needed but also feasible.

The death penalty—pro or con, right or wrong—is a moral question, perfectly resistant to scientific or statistical resolution, as centuries of debate have proven. Post-Cold War Europe has dealt with this conundrum by removing the issue from the normal scope of national sovereignty and democratic politics. The European Union defines capital punishment as a human rights issue under international law. It says everyone has an absolute right not to be put to death by the state, regardless of his crime, and regardless of the consequences of not executing him. No state that wishes to become or remain a part of the E.U. and to enjoy the many benefits of membership may practice capital punishment, even if its own citizens wish otherwise. Indeed, the E.U. arrived at this position despite strong residual support for capital punishment among European electorates.

The United States, by contrast, still deals with capital punishment in the framework of a sovereign representative democracy, whose institutions strive to express the majority's will while respecting both minority views and individual rights. Moreover, the U.S. is a federal republic in which all 50 states retain authority to keep the death penalty or abolish it within their borders, while Congress has that authority within its national jurisdiction. Through this decentralized dual system, the American people have a say on capital punishment, untrammeled by international law or supranational authority. In fact, they have multiple ways to have their say.

Unlike Europeans, Americans, through their representatives, retain the power of life and death. If this book advocates anything, it is that we acknowledge that power and use it wisely.

ONE

The Disappearance of Death?

oes the recent decline in the frequency of death sentences and executions presage the end of capital punishment in America, as the Texas official fears and global death penalty foes fervently hope? There is no denying the possibility. Over the course of history, the U.S. commitment to the death penalty has waxed and waned. At one point in the not-so-distant past, capital punishment very nearly did disappear in this country. Just over 40 years ago, in 1968, U.S. execution chambers shut down. That year, not a single prisoner was put to death in the entire country. It was an unprecedented moment in the twentieth century, and it culminated a long and steady decline in capital punishment that had actually begun about two decades earlier in the aftermath of World War II.

One way to assess the origins and causes of the death penalty's current decline is to compare and contrast it with this remarkable but, by now, mostly forgotten episode. Is history repeating itself, perhaps with a different final chapter this time around?

❧

The three decades following the Second World War were a time of great social and political turmoil in the United States: a revolution in civil rights and race relations; a struggle over communism at home and abroad; and the rise of new mass media as sources of values and arbiters of celebrity. Each of these trends had its corresponding death penalty drama: the plight of black men on death row in the South, who were frequently put to death for purported rapes of white women; the 1953 electrocution of atomic spy Julius Rosenberg and his wife, Ethel; and the campaign to spare Caryl Chessman, a charismatic and press-savvy sex offender who published several popular books while on death row, recasting himself as a brilliant rebel before dying in the California gas chamber in 1960.

Amid these events, popular support for capital punishment plummeted. In 1953, when the Gallup Poll asked Americans whether they favored the death penalty for murder, 68 percent said yes. Just 4 years later, in 1957, only 47 percent said yes; 34 percent said no. By 1966, only 42 percent favored the death penalty while 47 percent opposed it. This was the first time in the Gallup Poll's history that opposition to the death penalty exceeded support for it.[1]

The number of death sentences, especially in the North but also in the South, steadily declined in the two decades after World War II as jurors became less likely to sentence offenders to death and voters were less likely to punish elected officials who did not pursue capital punishment. Whereas an average of 142 people had been sentenced to death annually between 1935 and 1942, only 113 were sentenced to death each year during the 1960s.[2] On a per capita basis, death sentences were even less frequent because the U.S. population increased substantially. During this period, eight states abolished or drastically limited the death penalty legislatively: Alaska, Hawaii, Delaware (albeit for only 3 years, 1958 to 1961), Oregon, Iowa, West Virginia, Vermont, and New York.

Executions per year plunged even faster than sentences. They declined from a post-war peak of 153 in 1947 to 105 in 1951, 56 in 1960, 7 in 1965, and finally, none in 1968.[3] But the decline in executions had a distinct cause: changing attitudes within the courts. Chief Justice Earl Warren and an activist Supreme Court embarked on a broad campaign to rid the legal system of racial discrimination, police brutality, and other longstanding defects such as states' failure to guarantee defendants adequate legal counsel. By interpreting constitutional rights more broadly, the Warren Court gave criminal defendants, including those on death row, new ways to appeal convictions and sentences. It also gave them more procedural latitude to pursue those appeals, especially through habeas corpus petitions in federal court.

The resulting additional litigation slowed the pace of executions well beyond what the drop in sentences would have caused. The median amount of time spent on death row before having a sentence overturned grew from 19 months in 1961 to 41 months in 1967. And death row denizens were winning their cases at a rate of 43 per year, canceling out more than a third of the new death sentences annually.[4]

࿇

As in the previous era of decline, changes in public opinion may also explain some of today's decline in death sentences. Now, as then, apparent inequities and mistakes in the administration of capital punishment are in the forefront of public discussion. As in the past, much of the concern revolves around racial disparities, albeit in a new way. Studies show that white and black defendants are no longer sentenced to death at different rates, when all the relevant variables are taken into account. But statistical studies do consistently show that those who kill whites are more likely to get the death penalty than those who kill blacks.

As powerful as the racial disparity claim is, the most potent new charge against capital punishment is the "actual innocence" of some death-sentenced offenders. When justice misfires and an innocent man goes to prison, that mistake can eventually be corrected. Unique among all punishments, however, death is irrevocable. Thus, many Americans were troubled by the widely reported cases of several people sent to death row but later exonerated when modern DNA analysis of physical evidence proved they were not guilty. Of the scandals over wrongful death sentences in the past decade, none was more disturbing—or had a wider impact on public opinion—than the reports of 13 men mistakenly convicted on capital charges in Illinois between 1987 and 1998. This news led then-Governor George Ryan, a Republican, to declare a moratorium on executions in January 2000, and to commute the sentences of all 167 death row inmates in that state in January 2003.[5] According to the Gallup Poll, 25 percent of those who opposed the death penalty in 2003 said they reached that conclusion because "persons may be wrongly convicted." This was more than double the percentage that expressed that concern in 1991.

By 2008, overall support for the death penalty had fallen by 16 points from its all-time high of 80 percent in September 1994. Death penalty opponents appear to have won at least one important point in the debate. Proponents of capital punishment insist it deters murder, but 64 percent of the public disagrees, according to the May 2006 Gallup Poll. This represents a major shift. As recently as 1985, 62 percent of Americans did believe that the death penalty is a deterrent. The experience of the previous two decades apparently persuaded them otherwise.

Claims of ineradicable racial disparities and wrongful convictions, as well as claims that the death penalty does not deter murder, influenced the decisions by the New Jersey and New Mexico legislatures to abolish capital punishment in 2007 and 2008, respectively. In 2005, New York's state legislature declined to reinstate the death penalty after the New York Court of Appeals, the state's highest court, struck down its capital punishment statute the previous year. In declining to overturn the court ruling, New York legislators also reflected concerns about race, innocence, and non-deterrence. Their decision marked a decided change from 2002, when they had actually expanded eligibility for the death penalty in the aftermath of the September 11, 2001 terrorist attack on Manhattan.

Politicians in these three states clearly did not fear a voter backlash. Citizens aware of miscarriages of justice and other problems also may be less likely to impose death when they sit on juries. Prosecutors may be less willing to ask for it in marginal cases—especially now that all death penalty states, as well as the federal government and the U.S. military, offer the alternative sentence of life in prison without the possibility of parole. Only "death-qualified" jurors—those willing to impose the death penalty if they consider it warranted—sit on capital cases. Yet even many death-qualified jurors have qualms when the question is not death in the abstract but death for a particular person in a particular case. For an ambivalent juror, a non-lethal punishment that promises permanently to incapacitate a murderer can be an attractive alternative. In May 2006, the Gallup Poll gave respondents a choice between sentencing a convicted killer to death and sentencing him to life with "absolutely no possibility of parole." The two penalties finished in a statistical tie: 48 percent chose life without parole (LWOP) and 47 percent chose death.

That trend was reflected in Ohio, where a life without parole statute took effect in March 2005. That year, there were 16 capital murder indictments in Franklin County, Ohio—which includes Columbus and is the state's second-largest jurisdiction, with 1.1 million inhabitants—and none resulted in a death sentence. Over the next 3 years, Franklin County prosecutors sought capital punishment a total of only 17 times without a single jury voting for death, according to the *Columbus Dispatch*.[6] The Ohio law's impact was perhaps particularly strong because it permitted prosecutors to seek life without parole without first asking for death, as had previously been required. For Ohio as a whole, the Associated Press reported, "the number of life without parole sentences rose by more than two-thirds in the three years since the law took effect compared with the three years before, when 45 inmates entered prison with the permanent life sentence."[7]

As in the 1950s and 1960s, executions have plummeted of late. And, as in that prior period, the Supreme Court is a major cause of the change. Most notably, the court has banned the death penalty for two categories of offenders. In a 2002 case, *Atkins v. Virginia*, the court voted 6–3 to forbid capital punishment for moderately mentally retarded offenders—defined as those with an IQ between 50 and 70 and other social and cognitive disabilities. Reversing a position it took in a different case 13 years earlier, the court held that such persons were intrinsically less culpable than others, and that executing them would therefore constitute "cruel and unusual punishment" in violation of the Eighth Amendment to the U.S. Constitution. The *Atkins* ruling created a new constitutional claim for those already on death row. Mental retardation is a matter of medical and psychological proof.

Therefore, even if *Atkins* does not actually spare every death row inmate who invokes it, it promises further execution delays by creating a new font of litigation, as inmates seek opportunities to show that they are too mentally deficient to be put to death.[8]

Three years later, in *Roper v. Simmons*, the court adopted similar reasoning to abolish the death penalty for juvenile offenders—those who committed their crimes under the age of eighteen. This decision, too, represented a change of position by the court.[9] In a separate, more technical vein, the court ruled in 2002 that certain state capital sentencing laws that left the final decision to a judge (or judges) violated the Sixth Amendment right to trial by jury. This created another new issue for death row inmates in several states, notably Florida, which had such sentencing systems.[10]

Especially significant was the Supreme Court's intervention in several cases raising objections to lethal injection, the principal method of execution in the U.S. Conceived as a humane alternative to hanging, gas, or electrocution, lethal injection came under attack after the turn of the twenty-first century from critics who argued that an undetected misapplication of the commonly employed "cocktail" of drugs could actually cause the prisoner excruciating pain before he succumbed. The court first had to determine whether and under what circumstances anyone on death row could bring such a claim to court; having made that determination, the justices took on the substantive question of whether lethal injection was indeed "cruel and unusual."

Though the Court finally answered "no" in April 2008, some 16 executions around the country had been put on hold pending its decision, in addition to others that had been delayed or halted altogether during earlier related litigation.[11] Thanks to the lethal injection issue, there was a de facto 9-month moratorium on executions from September 2007 until June 2008. Even after the court's ruling, a few death row inmates won lower-court stays of execution on separate lethal injection-related issues.

જેન્જ

For the most part, however, the differences are more impressive than the similarities when comparing the post-war death penalty decline and the current one. Start with public opinion. Today's anti-death penalty trend is not only more modest than that of the first two post-war decades, it is much more modest than is commonly believed. As we have seen, support for capital punishment in the Gallup Poll plunged 26 points between 1953 and 1967, leaving more people against the death penalty than for it. Nothing like this shift has occurred lately. Yes, pro-death penalty sentiment has fallen to 64 percent, after reaching 80 percent in 1994. But even 64 percent represents a 35 percent swing in favor of the death penalty since 1966. The 80 percent pro-death penalty figure recorded in 1994 was actually an anomaly, from which the subsequent drop represents a return to more normal levels. Current support for the death penalty is roughly the same as it was in 1976—that is, at the beginning of the modern era of capital punishment.[12]

Other Gallup findings illustrate even more dramatically the persistence of American support for capital punishment. In October 2008, 71 percent of respondents told Gallup that the death penalty was imposed either "about the right amount" or "not enough." This was roughly the same response as in 2001. Significantly, however, the "not enough" share of the total, 48 percent, had increased ten points since 2001. Also, the percentage of people who believed the death penalty was being imposed "too often" remained the same at 21 percent. All of the increase in the "not enough" response, therefore, came from a reduction in those who believed the country had "about the right amount" of capital punishment. Apparently, a tenth of the American public has noticed that the death penalty is waning, and disapproves.

As it was in the 1950s and 1960s, concern about the fairness and efficacy of the U.S. death penalty is strongest today among those best positioned to communicate their views to the public: lawyers, journalists, entertainers, and religious leaders. The late Supreme Court Justice Harry Blackmun set the pace shortly before his 1994 retirement when he came out against the death penalty in a written opinion. "I shall no longer tinker with the machinery of death," he declared.[13] Several other distinguished members of the bench, both federal and state, have voiced concerns. Since 1997, the American Bar Association has called for a nationwide moratorium on executions pending a study of the death penalty's shortcomings. The nation's leading editorial pages oppose executions; and capital punishment's defects are a staple subject on the news pages. Hollywood films such as *The Green Mile* and *Dead Man Walking*, the latter based on the best-selling book by Sister Helen Prejean, found wide audiences.

Even as American opinion leaders have increasingly opposed the death penalty, international pressure on the United States has mounted. International pressure was also a factor half a century ago when the Soviet Union and its allies decried the discriminatory treatment of black capital defendants in the American South, and mounted a huge campaign around the execution of the Rosenbergs. Anti-death penalty activists in the democratic West condemned U.S. executions of that era as well, especially that of Caryl Chessman, which the Vatican also opposed. Today, pressure from abroad is, if anything, more effective than it was in the past because information technology facilitates the efforts of non-governmental organizations and because the campaign to abolish the death penalty is untainted by Soviet propaganda. It is spearheaded now by the European Union, a multinational bloc of wealthy democratic states armed with a new body of international human rights law.

Yet the outpouring of criticism from prominent individuals and institutions, foreign and domestic, has barely dented the views of ordinary people. Some 54 percent of Americans believe the death penalty is applied "fairly," according to the October 2008 Gallup survey—

a slight increase since 2000. The last time Gallup asked about wrongful convictions and executions was in May 2006 and the public then showed remarkably little concern. Some two-thirds of those surveyed backed the death penalty, even though the same fraction believed an innocent person had been put to death within the previous 5 years. Fewer Americans expressed concern about wrongful executions in 2006 than in 2003. Two-thirds said wrongful executions are rare.

Americans may no longer believe the death penalty is a deterrent, but they want capital punishment anyway. As Gallup reported in 2008, support for the death penalty reflects the public's "concept of justice"—not necessarily its notion about what policies do or do not actually stop crime. According to a 2003 Gallup study, "close to half of Americans who supported the death penalty cited some aspect of retribution for the crime as the reason."[14]

There is little reason to suppose that this basic sentiment has changed since then. And the retributive rationale is not even necessarily limited to cases of murder—judging by public reaction to an April 2008 Supreme Court decision that struck down six state laws that made raping a child a capital offense. The court held that the country had set its face against capital punishment for non-lethal crimes, but the voters apparently disagreed. In a Quinnipiac Poll taken shortly after the ruling, 55 percent of respondents favored the death penalty for a person convicted of raping a child, while 38 percent opposed it.[15] An even better barometer of public sentiment may have been the presidential candidates' reaction to the ruling: both Democrat Barack Obama and Republican John McCain denounced it.

Nor should one overstate the popularity of life without parole. The 2006 Gallup Poll's statistical tie between life without parole and death was not only ambiguous but, seemingly, anomalous. It was the only time since 1985 that life without parole was more heavily favored than death in the Gallup Poll (albeit within its margin of error). In every other year but one during those two decades, at least 50 percent of the public preferred the death penalty. And though Gallup has not returned to the subject since 2006, a 2007 AP/Ipsos poll found that 52 percent favored death, while only 37 percent favored life in prison without parole (9 percent chose life in prison with a chance for parole). In 2008, the Quinnipiac Poll gave death the edge over life without parole, 47 percent to 44 percent.[16]

To be sure, the recent evidence from Franklin County, Ohio cited earlier in this chapter counters this impression. But a 2004 study by John Blume, Theodore Eisenberg, and Martin T. Wells reinforces it. The researchers, professors of law at Cornell University, found that the introduction of life without parole makes no predictable difference in the sentences juries hand out. In two death penalty states, Maryland and Indiana, LWOP was associated with a 50 percent decline in the death-sentencing rate over 5 years, as compared to the half-decade before the law. However, it was a different story in two other states. In Georgia, the death sentence rate stayed the same, and in Mississippi it went up slightly. "[W]e find little evidence that the availability of LWOP reduces death sentence rates," the study's authors concluded.[17]

While symbolically important, the abolition of the death penalty in New York, New Jersey, and New Mexico obviously occurred well after the downward trend in death sentences had begun. But it is also highly unlikely that they will affect the rate of sentences very much in the coming years. By the time these three states abolished the death penalty, they were death penalty jurisdictions in name only. When the New York Court of Appeals overturned the state's capital punishment law in 2004, only seven people sat on the state's death row; no one had been executed in the Empire State since the early 1960s. In the last quarter-century before abolition in New Jersey, the state had sentenced only eight men to death and executed none. New Mexico had executed one person in the 30 years before Governor Bill Richardson signed an abolition law in March 2009. The state's repeal was not retroactive, but it is hard to imagine that it will ever actually execute the two men left on death row.

In fact, none of these three jurisdictions is representative of the most committed pro-death penalty states—what might be called the death penalty "heartland" in the U.S. Rather, they are swing states, each of which has previously gone through a cycle of enactment and repeal in the past half-century. New York abolished capital punishment in 1965 and reinstated it in 1995. New Jersey abolished it in 1972, by means of a state Supreme Court ruling, only to reinstate it by legislative enactment in 1982. New Mexico previously abolished capital punishment in 1969, then reinstated it a decade later. In 1986, calling the death penalty "anti-God," the state's then-Governor Toney Anaya commuted the sentences of the five inmates on the state's death row to life in prison.

Notably, at roughly the same time that New Mexico was repealing the death penalty, the state legislature of Maryland was retaining it, in modified form, despite an all-out push for abolition by Governor Martin O'Malley. Meanwhile, in Wisconsin, which last executed someone in 1851, and which abolished the death penalty in 1853, the public appears to want to give capital punishment a try. A non-binding 2006 referendum showed that 56 percent of Wisconsin voters favored instituting the death penalty.[18]

The impact of the Supreme Court's 2002 *Atkins* ruling and 2005 *Roper* ruling is real but limited. By the time of *Atkins*, most death penalty states already exempted the mentally retarded from capital punishment, so few such persons were being sentenced to death in any case: Human Rights Watch estimated that there were between 200 and 300 possibly mentally retarded prisoners among what was then a death row population of 3,700.[19] Even assuming that the higher Human Rights Watch figure is accurate, and that mentally retarded offenders would have continued being sentenced to death at the same rate if *Atkins* had come out the other way, the case reduced future U.S. death sentences by at most eight percent. Death sentences for juvenile offenders were already on the way out when the court decided *Roper* in 2005; by that time, only 73 inmates were on death row for crimes they had committed before the age of eighteen.[20]

కళ

In Edgar Allan Poe's classic detective story, "The Purloined Letter," the Paris police fail to spot the crucial clue, a stolen envelope, even though it is hidden in plain sight. In the same way, the most important factor in the recent decline in U.S. death sentences is obvious, yet seems to have escaped the notice of most commentators. The shrinking death sentence rate is closely related to a steep plunge in the rate of violent crime, including the most common capital crime: murder. Declines in violent crime and murder affect capital punishment in two ways. First, and most directly, capital punishment decreases simply because there is less occasion for it. Second, but less directly, when people feel safer their belief in the death penalty seems less urgent. They may become more tolerant of anti-death penalty arguments. According to research by Katherine Y. Barnes at the University of Michigan Law School, the national violent crime rate is a good predictor of support for the death penalty. She reported in a 2002 paper that the violent crime rate explained approximately 70 percent of the yearly variation in public support for the death penalty between 1965 and 2000.[21]

History, including that of the 1950s and 1960s, lends support to this hypothesis. The current decline in the death penalty is actually the third such downturn in the past century or so. The first came at the outset of the twentieth century when elites, influenced by modern psychology and genetics, began to question the death penalty. The new sciences undermined traditional views about individual free will and, hence, individual culpability. This reconsideration took place amid a relatively low homicide rate, which fluctuated between four and six murders per 100,000 people in the years prior to World War I. Accordingly, many state legislatures eliminated the death penalty completely or partially; the number of executions fell from 161 in 1912 to 65 in 1919—the lowest count since 1869.[22]

But violence surged in the 1920s because Prohibition gave rise to organized crime. The murder rate, which had remained at about 6 homicides per 100,000 people through World War I, rose sharply to 9.7 homicides per

100,000 people by 1933.[23] High-minded theories about the limitations of individual responsibility gave way to a general fear of crime. The death penalty made a comeback. The year 1935 saw 199 executions, still the largest single-year total recorded in modern times.[24]

In 1933, however, the country ended Prohibition and the murder rate began a long-term decline. It bottomed out at 4.5 per 100,000 in 1955—the lowest figure since 1910—and stayed there for the next 4 years.[25] Indeed, the U.S. murder rate remained at low levels through the mid-1960s, not exceeding 5.5 per 100,000 until 1966, a year in which, not coincidentally, there were just two executions and support for capital punishment reached its all-time low in the Gallup Poll. The poll results reflected a long period of safe streets.

To be sure, low crime was not the only factor shaping attitudes about the death penalty, but it was a necessary factor. Without it, the post-World War II decline in the death penalty might not have happened, or, if it did, might have been much shallower.

Between 1965 and 1980, however, the murder rate nearly doubled, reaching a peak of 10.2 per 100,000 people. During the 1980s, the murder rate stayed well above the levels of the 1950s, fluctuating between 7.9 and 9.8 per

100,000.[26] Public support for capital punishment followed the murder rate's upward trajectory.

And then, much to the surprise of experts who had almost unanimously predicted the opposite, the tide of crime began to ebb. Between 1991 and 2000, the U.S. homicide rate fell 44 percent, from 9.8 to 5.5 per 100,000 people—the lowest rate in more than three decades. Every region of the country and all demographic groups benefitted from the trend, albeit not precisely equally. Moreover, the homicide rate has stayed down, remaining at or near 5.5 per 100,000 people ever since 2001.[27]

The "Great American Crime Decline," as criminologist Franklin Zimring has labeled it, is not yet well understood. Social scientists point to the decline of the violent "crack" cocaine trade, the hiring of thousands of police officers, and the incarceration of massive numbers of criminals for long periods. No one in the U.S. should be proud, or happy, about the fact that the state and federal prison population now exceeds two million people—or that a disproportionate number of the prisoners are black and Latino. The over-incarceration of non-violent drug offenders is a genuine concern. But bona fide violent criminals account for much of the recent growth of the state prison population, and harsh punishment of violent offenders has probably kept many of them from eventually becoming murderers, or deterred others from starting a life of crime. Notably, the same Supreme Court that abolished the death penalty for the mentally retarded and for juveniles has upheld draconian state laws that condemn some offenders to life in prison after their third felony conviction.[28]

For our purposes, however, the causes of the decline in crime are less important than the effects. To repeat: when there are fewer murders, there are fewer cases in which the states can seek the death penalty. Consistent with this common-sense notion, a comprehensive analysis by Cornell law professors Blume, Eisenberg, and Wells concluded in 2004 that "the number of murders [in a state] is the most important factor in explaining the number of death sentences."[29]

The Cornell study produced the surprising finding that, adjusted for its homicide rate, Texas was not the state with the highest propensity to sentence people to death. Instead, between 1977 and 1999, Texas sentenced murderers to death at a rate of 20 for every 1,000 homicides in the state, the median rate for all death penalty states in that interval. The most death sentence-prone state turned out to be Nevada, which sentenced murderers to death at the rate of 60 for every 1,000 homicides—triple Texas's rate. Pennsylvania and Ohio outranked Texas, too, contrary to much conventional wisdom. Also contrary to conventional wisdom, more than half of the top ten death-sentencing states were outside the South. To be sure, other variables, including the specific state-law provisions defining eligibility for the death penalty, the ideology of state judges, and the nature of political pressure on the courts, also affect the capital sentencing rate. But the study's authors concluded that the murder rate is still "the most important factor," even after taking these other variables into account.[30]

The nationwide decline in annual murder rates since 1991 accounts for well over half of the decline in death sentences per year. Indeed, nationally, the drop in the prior year's murder rate accounts for two-thirds of the decline in the annual number of death sentences between 1992 and 2008. The pattern is especially clear in Texas, the world-famous stronghold of the death penalty. In 1992, the state's homicide rate reached a truly frightening 12.7 per 100,000, and then began to fall. By 2007, it was down to 5.9 per 100,000, a decline of 53.5 percent. Between 1993 and 2008, death sentences per year declined 64 percent, from 34 to 13. In other words, for Texas, the decline in prior-year homicides accounts for 84 percent of the decline in annual death sentences.

Death Sentences and Homicides per 100,000 Residents in Texas, 1991-2008

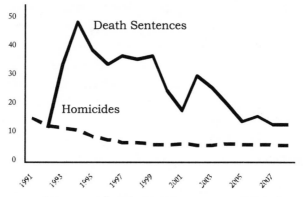

Source: U.S. Department of Justice, Bureau of Justice Statistics, "State level homicide trends and characteristics," http://bjs-data.ojp.usdoj.gov/dataonline/Search/Homicide/State/State-Homicide.cfm (accessed April 16, 2009); Death Penalty Information Center, "Death Sentences in the United States, 1977-2007, http://www.deathpenaltyinfo.org/death-sentences-united-states-1977-2007 (accessed May 9, 2009).

This relationship among declining and/or low murder rates, public opinion, and capital punishment policy helps explain why the U.S. experienced declines in the death penalty both during the two post-war decades and during the past decade and a half. But it also may explain the fact that the decline during the 1950s and 1960s was so much steeper than the current one. To be sure, the death penalty had farther to fall in the earlier of the two periods, in the sense that the sentencing rate was higher at the outset than it was even at the recent peak in 1998.

Still, it seems probable that public support dropped more steeply between the early 1950s and the mid-1960s than it has since 1994 because the murder rate was so low during the earlier time. Conversely, it is doubtful that support for capital punishment can be depressed much more today without a considerable, sustained reduction in violent crime.

Indeed, this cyclical dynamic—and the failure of the anti-death penalty movement to acknowledge it—helps explain the ultimate collapse of the de facto moratorium on capital punishment that prevailed from 1968 through 1976. In the early 1960s, death penalty abolitionist lawyers, led by the Legal Defense Fund of the National Association for the Advancement of Colored People (LDF), embarked on constitutional litigation aimed at the same sort of Supreme Court ruling against capital punishment that the LDF had won against school segregation in *Brown v. Board of Education.* Encouraged by the Warren Court's approach to criminal justice issues, the lawyers argued that racial and other disparities rendered the death penalty so arbitrary as to qualify as "cruel and unusual punishment." There was an irony in their argument, of course, since it hinged on the increasingly infrequent—"unusual"—imposition of the death penalty, which in turn reflected legal victories by anti-death penalty litigators.

Nevertheless, in 1972 a plurality of the Supreme Court agreed with the LDF and ruled that all state capital punishment laws were unconstitutional. All nine justices submitted written opinions in the case, *Furman v. Georgia.* Their views ran the gamut, with two justices embracing outright abolition of the death penalty and four voting to uphold it. But the controlling view, expressed in Justice Potter Stewart's opinion, was that existing state laws did not give juries enough guidance in deciding whether to choose the death penalty, making it "cruel and unusual in the same way that being struck by lightning is cruel and unusual."[31] The ruling cleared death row.

Thus did the court seek to make permanent the fadeout of capital punishment that had brought executions to zero by 1968. But, as a barometer of the country's mood, the execution rate was misleading; the court had chosen the wrong moment for its initiative. Actually, the liberal atmosphere of the early '60s was waning, in large part because of an upsurge in crime. The murder rate nearly doubled between 1965 and 1972, the year of *Furman*, when it reached 9.4 per 100,000. This was alarmingly close to the previous record set in 1933. (In 1974, the murder rate reached 10.1 per 100,000.) The public clamored for "law and order," and Richard Nixon's promise to deliver it helped propel him to the White House in 1968 and to re-election in 1972.

In this atmosphere, *Furman* seemed to increase rather than decrease pro-death penalty sentiment. In March 1972, shortly before the *Furman* ruling, the Gallup Poll reported that death penalty supporters outnumbered opponents 50 to 42 percent. By November of that year, after *Furman*, the margin had grown: 57 percent favored the death penalty and 32 percent opposed it—that is, an 8-point gap had grown to a 25-point gap.[32] On Election Day, California's voters approved a pro-death penalty referendum by a 2–1 margin. The numbers reflected not only greater approval of the death penalty, but also the fact that Americans did not like the way in which the Supreme Court had encroached on the power of the states to make their own policy.

The backlash against *Furman* was swift and strong. Most states, 35 in all, rewrote their death penalty laws to answer Potter Stewart's objections. And in 1976, when the LDF's inevitable challenges to these statutes reached the Supreme Court, the justices upheld the new laws. The controlling plurality opinion in the case, *Gregg v. Georgia*, written by Stewart, Lewis F. Powell (appointed by Nixon), and John Paul Stevens (appointed by President Gerald R. Ford), all but acknowledged that the court was bowing to the backlash against *Furman*. "Despite the continuing debate, dating back to the 19th century, over the morality and utility of capital punishment," the opinion read, "it is now evident that a large proportion of American society continues to regard it as an appropriate and necessary criminal sanction . . . The most marked indication of society's endorsement of the death penalty for murder is the legislative response to *Furman*."[33]

In 1977, Gary Gilmore of Utah became the first American executed in a decade. Death row reopened and began to fill again. The last gasp of the LDF's attempt to end the death penalty through constitutional litigation came in 1987. The Supreme Court in a 5–4 vote rejected the LDF's claim that the death penalty was racially biased because killers of whites in Georgia were more likely to be sentenced to death than killers of blacks. A leading opponent of the death penalty wrote later that *Furman* "may have helped to bring the trend away from capital punishment to a premature end."[34]

There was, it turned out, no judicial shortcut to abolition; the Supreme Court could not impose its views on an unwilling public. We will never know what might have happened if death penalty opponents had pursued a different course. Other factors, especially the rising crime rate, probably would have brought the death penalty back in some form. Still, it is entirely possible that, over the long run, there would have been less capital punishment without *Furman.* It is an irony both opponents and supporters of the death penalty would do well to ponder.

TWO

The Case Against the Case Against the Death Penalty

The death penalty is a grim business: the deliberate, pre-meditated killing of a human being by government officials. They can accomplish this by hanging, electrocution, or, as in the vast majority of U.S. cases today, lethal injection—but they can never make it pretty. They certainly cannot make it perfect. And if it comes to executing the wrong person, that error would be irreversible. As conservative columnist George

Will has put it, "Capital punishment, like the rest of the criminal justice system, is a government program, so skepticism is in order."[1]

Of course, the anti-death penalty movement believes not only that the death penalty is grotesque and error-prone, but that it is morally wrong, and that even a smoothly functioning, bias-free death penalty would violate basic human decency and basic human rights. In the years since *Furman* and *Gregg*, however, abolitionists have downplayed moral arguments. Having lost the battle for a judicial override of the public's pro-death penalty sentiment, the anti-death penalty movement retreated to a more defensible line: that the obstacles to an equitable, accurate death penalty in the United States are insurmountable.

This pragmatic case against capital punishment is probably more effective than the purely moral case would have been. It does not require anyone to embrace the abolitionist moral argument. You can be against the death penalty as it exists in the U.S. today without necessarily deciding whether you would be against the death penalty in any and all circumstances. Furthermore, the pragmatic case rests on two powerful empirical claims. First: racial disparities in capital sentencing are both an historical and a contemporary reality in the

United States. Second: capital punishment, by its nature, risks wrongful execution, a risk that cannot easily be reconciled with U.S. standards of due process—and that may actually have materialized in the past.

These are anything but trivial concerns. The question, however, is whether the race and innocence problems are actually as large and as ineradicable as the anti-death penalty movement maintains. My answer is a qualified "no." While real, both issues have been overstated; neither poses an insuperable obstacle to death penalty reform. While claims of widespread racial bias and wrongful convictions have convinced some Americans that the death penalty cannot work, overreliance on—and exaggeration of—these claims may have repelled others.

◈◈

Anyone who doubts the death penalty's past connection with racism in the United States need only consider the following statistics. Between 1930 and 1967, 54 percent of the 3,859 people put to death under civilian authority in the U.S. were African American.[2] This was not only out of proportion with the black share of the total population—roughly 11 percent during this period—but also out of proportion with the percentage of serious crimes committed by blacks. Of course, the skewed statistics reflected the fact that states in the South used the death penalty to enforce a broader caste system. In particular, Southern states put blacks to death for the crime of rape far more often than whites, especially when the alleged victim was a white woman. Of the 455 men executed for rape in the United States between 1930 and 1967, 90 percent were African American.[3]

These appalling facts formed the background for the Supreme Court's consideration of the death penalty in the 1960s and 1970s. It was no accident that the LDF, the preeminent civil rights litigation organization of the day, brought the cases that culminated in *Furman v. Georgia*. Two of the three cases grouped under that title actually involved appeals by African American men sentenced to death for raping white women in the South. The third was a black man convicted of killing a white man in the course of a bungled burglary.

To be sure, the Supreme Court did not explicitly confront racial disparities during this period; it refused even to hear the LDF's argument that the discriminatory death penalty for rape violated the constitutional guarantee of equal treatment under state law.[4] However, in *Furman*, at least one justice in the majority, William O. Douglas, opined that racial disparities were part of what made the death penalty cruel and unusual, and other justices alluded to race in their analyses of the penalty's arbitrariness. "Race discrimination was not formally part of *Furman*, and Douglas was the only justice who emphasized it," writes Professor Stuart Banner of the University of California at Los Angeles law school, a death penalty historian. "But everyone knew it was lurking not far beneath the surface."[5]

Furman therefore left room for states to try to purge their capital punishment laws of the caprice that troubled the swing voters on the court. The states did so by requiring juries to weigh the defendant's sentence separately from his guilt or innocence, and, in this "sentencing trial," to take account of both "aggravating" evidence that supported the death penalty and "mitigating" evidence that argued against it. And in *Gregg*, the court approved of such sentencing schemes, with the three-justice plurality concluding that, in light of society's obvious approval of capital punishment, statutes that guided the jury's discretion could be constitutional. As the *Gregg* plurality put it, the laws "narrowed the class of murderers subject to capital punishment," thus curing the ills the court had identified in *Furman*. "[W]here discretion is afforded a sentencing body on a matter so grave as the determination of whether a human life should be taken or spared, that discretion must be suitably directed and limited so as to minimize the risk of wholly arbitrary and capricious action," they wrote.[6]

Though usually remembered as the court's failed attempt to abolish the death penalty, *Furman* nevertheless had a lasting impact, rendering capital punishment less blatantly racist than it had been in the past. Most new state laws adopted in response to *Furman* omitted rape as a capital crime. *Gregg* provided at least some assurance that jurors would consider an individual defendant's disadvantages in life, including those related to racial discrimination. Even more importantly, perhaps, *Gregg* created a basis for condemned men to claim on appeal that their sentencers had failed to consider such "mitigating" factors. And finally, the court followed up *Gregg* in 1977 by banning the death penalty for rape of an adult woman, albeit in a decision that emphasized not race but society's evolving notions of the appropriate punishment for such crimes. Though only Georgia still prescribed death for rape at that point, the court seemed determined to make sure it never came back.[7]

These changes helped remake the racial composition of death row. Whereas some 54 percent of those executed between 1930 and 1967 were black, as we have seen, 56 percent of those executed in the post-*Gregg* era have been white, while 35 percent have been black and 9 percent have been Latinos and other racial minorities. In other words, the African American share of executions dropped by a third. Whites also make up the largest portion of those *sentenced* to death during this period.[8]

To be sure, this did not necessarily mean that racial imbalances had been eliminated. African Americans were still overrepresented on death row, relative to their share of the population. And, in the aftermath of *Gregg*, death penalty critics discovered a different—but to them no less troubling—racial pattern in sentencing. The disparity involved not the race of the defendant, but the race of the victim. In a famous LDF-funded study of 2,484 murder cases in Georgia between 1973 and 1979, Professor David Baldus of the University of Iowa showed that, even after taking account of 39 non-racial variables, defendants charged with killing whites were 4.3 times as likely to receive the death penalty as defendants charged with killing blacks. And, within the category of those who killed whites, black defendants were 10 percent more likely to receive a death sentence than were whites.[9]

Armed with the Baldus study, the LDF took another shot at persuading the Supreme Court that the death penalty was hopelessly infected with arbitrary considerations such as race, even in Georgia, whose new statute the court had specifically approved in *Gregg*. Of course, the argument had extra plausibility in a Southern state that had recently emerged from a racist past, and whose jurors, prosecutors, and judges were thus presumably still susceptible to racism, even if it was less overt. To the LDF, Baldus's statistics showed that, consciously or not, Georgia's legal apparatus placed a higher value on white life than black life, and thus punished murder of whites more harshly than murder of blacks, especially when a black man had the effrontery to kill a white person.

In a 1987 case, *McCleskey v. Kemp*, the court rejected this claim by a vote of 5–4. For the majority, Justice Lewis F. Powell wrote that the LDF had failed to show any discriminatory intent on the part of Georgia officials, and that without such a showing, the court could not infer unconstitutional motives from Baldus's statistics. "We decline to assume that what is unexplained is invidious," Justice Powell wrote. "Although the history of racial discrimination in this country is undeniable, we cannot accept official actions taken long ago as evidence of current intent." To hold otherwise, Justice Powell added, would potentially undermine the entire justice system by rendering unconstitutional any statistical disparity in sentencing, capital or otherwise, among ethnic groups, men and women, or even attractive defendants and unattractive ones.[10]

McCleskey foreclosed constitutional challenges based on statistics such as those in Baldus's study, but it could not stop Baldus and others from continuing their research. They went on to produce more and more studies showing similar race-of-the-victim disparities in states across the country. This pattern is so well-documented that not even supporters of capital punishment spend much time disputing it anymore. As a result, *McCleskey* has acquired a bad reputation, with some legal academics putting it in the same category as the 1857 *Dred Scott* decision that said people of African ancestry could not claim U.S. citizenship. After retiring from the court, Justice Powell himself told a biographer that he regretted his opinion in the *McCleskey* case.[11]

But Justice Powell may have been excessively self-critical. Though recent statistical research confirms Baldus's observations, it does not necessarily support the interpretation of the data that death penalty opponents advanced in *McCleskey*—and still advance today. The fact that killers of whites are more likely to receive the death penalty does not necessarily reflect racism of the kind that pervaded the pre-*Furman* system; it does not necessarily reflect racism at all. To the contrary, in some instances it appears to reflect racial progress.

This more differentiated assessment of the role of race in the modern death penalty begins by acknowledging that African Americans commit a disproportionate number of murders in the U.S.: approximately half, according to government statistics.[12] Yet, in the death penalty states of post-*Gregg* America, black murderers have been somewhat *less* likely to wind up on death row than their white counterparts. Cornell law professors Blume, Eisenberg, and Wells note that blacks committed 51.5 percent of murders nationwide between 1976 and 1998, but accounted for only 41.3 percent of those sentenced to death from 1977 to 1999. This relationship held true in every death penalty state, and—contrary to conventional wisdom—the under-representation of blacks on death row was greatest in the South. Only California, Utah, and Nevada came close to sentencing black murderers to death in proportion to their share of the total.[13]

The Cornell law professors (who oppose the death penalty) confirmed Baldus's research in the sense that they also detected what they called "a racial hierarchy" in capital sentencing. Blacks charged with killing blacks were sentenced to death less often than whites charged with killing whites, and blacks charged with killing whites were sentenced to death most frequently of all.

Race, however, "tugs in two different directions," they argued. The higher likelihood of a death sentence for black killers of whites tends to increase the black share of death row. The lower likelihood of a death sentence for black killers of blacks tends to decrease it. And the second effect is far larger than the first, since blacks are far more likely to kill other blacks than they are to kill whites. As the Cornell law professors put it, "Interracial crime is the exception, not the rule." Therefore, the relative lack of black killers of blacks on death row "swamps" the relative excess of black killers of whites and largely explains the under-representation of black murderers among those sentenced to death.[14]

That leaves the question of why black-on-black murder so seldom results in the death penalty. One possibility is that these killings are less likely than others to take place during the commission of an additional crime, such as rape, robbery, or kidnapping, which is the usual standard for aggravated or capital murder under state death penalty statutes. According to recent data assembled by the non-profit Violence Policy Center in Washington, D.C., black-victim homicides rarely include additional crimes. In 2006, for example, there was no other felony in 69 percent of the black-victim homicides for which the circumstances could be identified. The typical scenario, the study showed, was an argument between friends, family members, or acquaintances that escalated until someone impulsively reached for a gun and shot the victim.[15]

According to the Cornell law professors, the main factor in this equation is the reluctance of local prosecutors to seek the death penalty in black-on-black homicides. What accounts for that reluctance? While not dismissing the possibility that white prosecutors—consciously or not—placed a lower value on black life, the Cornell professors emphasized another reason: prosecutorial realism. Above all, prosecutors do not seek the death penalty unless they think they can actually persuade a jury to impose it.[16] In jurisdictions with large African American populations, where most black-on-black crime occurs, persuading a jury to sentence a defendant to death is relatively difficult. As much survey data confirms, African Americans are the one U.S. demographic group that largely opposes the death penalty, no doubt because of its terrible historical impact on blacks in the South.[17] Also, in jurisdictions where elected prosecutors must appeal to black voters, prosecutors are that much less likely to support capital punishment.

This is how race-of-the-victim disparities can be said to reflect racial progress. After all, blacks neither voted in elections nor served on juries in substantial numbers, especially in the South, until the late 1960s. Now that they do, they appear to be using this power to limit capital punishment in the cases closest to them.

Theodore Eisenberg of Cornell law school found support for this hypothesis in a study of county-level data for five death penalty states—Georgia, Maryland, Pennsylvania, South Carolina, and Virginia—which he published in 2005. The study showed that the death sentence rate in black defendant / black victim homicides decreases as the percentage of blacks in a county's population increases. "This suggests that minority community skepticism about the justness of the death penalty is a contributing factor to low death sentence rates" in black-on-black murder cases, Eisenberg concluded.[18]

Maryland presents a particularly suggestive case study. Its pre-*Furman* death penalty practices resembled those of the South. A significant portion of its executions prior to 1972—about a third—came in rape cases. Maryland re-established the death penalty after *Gregg* in a 1978 statute that omitted the death penalty for rape and specified first-degree murder with certain aggravating factors as the only death-eligible crime. Since then, Maryland has not been a major locus of the death penalty; despite its relatively high murder rate, the state sentenced only 66 murderers to death after 1978. Of those, only five were eventually executed (the first in 1994) and five remain on death row.[19]

The other thing that happened in post-*Gregg* Maryland was the rise of black majorities in the city of Baltimore and in Prince George's County, a suburb of Washington, D.C. These two jurisdictions account for the vast majority of homicides in the state, most of which involve both black victims and perpetrators. Yet public officials in both jurisdictions have generally eschewed the death penalty, consistent with their own views and the views of their constituents (who are also potential jurors). Baltimore city prosecutors last sought and won the death penalty in 1998 in a single case that was later overturned on appeal. The last Prince George's County death sentence occurred in 1996.[20]

The situation could not have been more different in Baltimore County, a 75 percent white suburb adjacent to the city of Baltimore. During most of the post-*Gregg* period, the county's chief prosecutor adhered to a policy of seeking the death penalty in every eligible case. Ironically enough, she did so to avoid any appearance of racial discrimination; her view was that she could never be accused of exercising prosecutorial discretion in a discriminatory manner if she never exercised it at all.[21]

Given Baltimore County's relatively large population (750,000 in 2005) and its white majority—which meant that most homicide victims were white—and given the polar opposite policies pursued by its black-majority neighbors, it is no wonder that Maryland's death penalty was meted out more frequently to killers of whites. But this was a consequence of county-level politics and demography, not statewide racial discrimination. Indeed, much if not most of the racial and jurisdictional imbalance in Maryland's death penalty demonstrates the increased power of black citizens during the post-*Gregg* era. Most African Americans in Maryland, like most African Americans generally, oppose the death penalty; and where they live, it has been abolished de facto.

❧

Innocence is the death penalty's Achilles Heel. No system of capital punishment can offer an absolute guarantee against miscarriages of justice. And no miscarriage of justice would be more awful and more irreparable than one resulting in the killing, by the government, of an innocent person. As U.S. District Judge Michael Ponsor of Massachusetts has written, "A legal regime relying on the death penalty will inevitably execute innocent people—not too often, one hopes, but undoubtedly sometimes. Mistakes will be made because it is simply not possible to do something this difficult perfectly, all the time. Any honest proponent of capital punishment must face this fact."[22]

The inherent risk of a mistaken execution has always been a part of the case against the death penalty, both in the U.S. and elsewhere. Indeed, when Great Britain abolished the death penalty in 1969, it did so in part because of a long controversy over an alleged wrongful execution, that of convicted murderer James Hanratty, who went to the gallows in 1962 insisting that he was innocent.

But the risk of wrongful execution was not an especially salient argument against the death penalty in the U.S. until after *Mc-Cleskey*. That case marked the defeat of constitutional litigation based on arguments about race and fairness, and forced capital punishment opponents to find new ones. Claiming that government cannot be trusted to find and convict the right person every time was such an argument—both because it is logical and because it resonates in a political culture already skeptical of the authorities.

Modern technology propelled "innocence" to the front pages. In 1993, DNA analysis of forensic evidence proved the innocence of Kirk Bloodsworth, who had been sentenced to death for murder in Maryland. Then came the scandal over mistaken convictions in Illinois, which prompted then-Governor George Ryan to impose a moratorium on executions in 2000.

Michael L. Radelet, chair of the sociology department at the University of Colorado at Boulder and a veteran academic opponent of the death penalty, argues that while "the innocence argument" cannot account for the entire decline in the death penalty in recent years, it has "changed attitudes" and even reopened debate over "the morality of the death penalty as applied by an imperfect criminal justice system."[23]

If federal court opinions are any indication, Radelet has a point. In April 2002, Judge Jed Rakoff of the U.S. District Court in Manhattan held the federal death penalty unconstitutional. "The best available evidence," he wrote, "indicates that, on the one hand, innocent people are sentenced to death with materially greater frequency than was previously supposed and that, on the other hand, convincing proof of their innocence often does not emerge until long after their convictions."[24]

In 2005, Supreme Court Justice David Souter echoed Rakoff. The occasion was the case of *Kansas v. Marsh*, which posed a relatively technical challenge to Kansas's death penalty statute. By a vote of 5–4, the court upheld the Kansas law. But Souter, joined by three other liberal justices, took the occasion to deliver a dissenting opinion in which he rehearsed evidence about false guilty verdicts in capital cases, arguing that "the Illinois experience shows them to be remarkable in number and . . . probably disproportionately high in capital cases." According to Souter, "we are thus in a period of new empirical argument about how 'death is different'" from other penalties.[25]

Souter's colleague, Justice Antonin Scalia, fired back with an opinion charging, correctly, that "the dissent does not discuss a single case—not one—in which it is clear that a person was executed for a crime he did not commit." Death row exonerations or executive clemency, Scalia argued, "demonstrate not the failure of the system but its success" since the end result was to avoid the actual execution of an innocent man. Acknowledging that no system could be perfect, Scalia nonetheless concluded, based on his own reading of the literature, that the possibility of a wrongful execution has "been reduced to an insignificant minimum" in the United States.[26]

Who has the better of the "empirical argument" to which Souter alluded? Consider the impact of DNA. The individual cases of exoneration are heartbreaking. Earl Washington of Virginia and Ray Krone of Arizona sat in prison for 19 and 11 years respectively before DNA set them free. One of the most disturbing exonerations was that of Frank Lee Smith, who served 14 years on death row in Florida for a rape-murder he swore he did not commit. Smith died of cancer in 2000 while incarcerated. His appeals were still pending. Posthumous DNA testing proved that he was indeed innocent.[27]

Yet actual numbers of DNA exonerations are not nearly as large as Rakoff and Souter implied. According to data compiled by the Death Penalty Information Center (DPIC), a leading anti-death penalty nonprofit organization in Washington, D.C., a total of 17 people sentenced to death have been later exonerated with the help of DNA evidence in the post-*Gregg* era. Troubling as they are, even these seemingly clear-cut cases can be overstated. Kirk Bloodsworth, for example, did not quite belong on the DPIC list since he was not actually on death row when his DNA exoneration occurred. In fact, Bloodsworth had already appealed and won a new trial in which, though he was again wrongly convicted of murder, his sentence was set at life in prison. So he was not facing the prospect of execution in 1993 when DNA evidence set him free. The same is true for Earl Washington and Ray Krone, whose death sentences had been voided as of the time DNA helped exonerate them.[28]

If Bloodsworth is the avatar of innocence, Roger Coleman has come to embody the anti-death penalty movement's occasional over-reaching. Coleman, from Grundy, Virginia, was convicted and sentenced to death for the 1981 rape and stabbing of his 19-year-old sister-in-law Wanda McCoy. For years thereafter, he insisted on his innocence. A campaign blossomed to set him free, reminiscent of the one on behalf of Caryl Chessman a generation before. Coleman was interviewed on national television and his face appeared on the cover of *Time* under the headline, "This Man Might Be Innocent. This Man is Due to Die." Coleman's supporters even publicly named another man as the guilty party. As Virginia officials strapped him into the electric chair in 1992, he declared that "an innocent man is going to be murdered tonight."[29]

DNA tests in 1990 had incriminated Coleman, but after his execution his supporters insisted that a new test using more modern technology would have exonerated him. In 2000, the Virginia Supreme Court denied their request for a re-examination of the evidence. Six years later, then-Governor Mark Warner of Virginia allowed the more advanced test, which confirmed that Coleman had indeed committed murder.[30]

Coleman's was not an isolated case. Convicted of murdering and raping a 17-year-old college student in Virginia in 1993, Derek Rocco Barnabei insisted on his innocence and became a cause célèbre in his ancestral Italy. Professor Alan Dershowitz of Harvard Law School proclaimed the Barnabei case "one of the most egregious miscarriages of justice and one of the most compelling cases of innocence I have ever seen in all my years of practicing law." After his conviction, Barnabei demanded that the state perform DNA tests on blood found under the victim's fingernails, which it had failed to do before his trial. Instead of proving that another man committed the crime, as Barnabei had insisted, the DNA test confirmed Barnabei's guilt. Virginia executed him in 2000.[31]

James Hanratty also had his guilt confirmed by posthumous collection of DNA evidence. Granting an appeal by Hanratty's family, the British government exhumed his corpse and gathered genetic material to compare with material from the crime scene. DNA testing confirmed that Hanratty was indeed the author of the crime, a fact that a British court reaffirmed in a 2002 ruling.[32]

In short, DNA is a double-edged sword. It can set innocent men free, but it can also reinforce society's confidence in guilty verdicts, including the validity of capital verdicts. The backlog of older cases that pre-date the existence of DNA technology has now been nearly cleared with no proof that anyone from that period was wrongly executed, as opposed to wrongly convicted. From here on out, when DNA evidence exists it will presumably be evaluated before a suspect is even charged, thus increasing the reliability of capital trials. To that extent, the concerns of Rakoff and Souter, both of whom perceived a growing problem of actual innocence, have been overtaken by events.

To be sure, many claims of actual innocence do not revolve around DNA. Sometimes a death row inmate produces testimony from witnesses who either did not testify at trial or who recant past incriminating testimony. These claims should also be treated with caution, as the case of John W. Byrd Jr. of Ohio illustrates. Convicted of stabbing a convenience store clerk to death in 1981, Byrd fought execution for two decades, insisting he had been asleep in a van outside while two accomplices actually robbed the store and killed the clerk. He was aided in his effort by an affidavit from one of the accomplices, serving life in prison, who claimed from his cell that he, not Byrd, had done the actual killing.

As the country reeled from terrorist attacks on September 11, 2001, Byrd convinced the U.S. Court of Appeals for the Sixth Circuit in Cincinnati to grant an extraordinary last-minute stay of execution, followed by an equally unusual opportunity to present his case at a hearing before a U.S. magistrate judge. There was a relative paucity of physical evidence linking Byrd to the crime, and Judge Nathaniel Jones of the Sixth Circuit, a veteran opponent of capital punishment, had been persuaded of Byrd's probable innocence. At Jones' urging, a majority of the judges on the Sixth Circuit bent the usual rules of procedure to stave off what they feared would be a wrongful execution.

But at the evidentiary hearing, Byrd's case crumbled. It became clear that his lawyers had misled the court and concealed relevant evidence, and that one of Byrd's alibi witnesses had been coached by Byrd's sister shortly before they had a sexual encounter. The magistrate not only rejected Byrd's claim of innocence; he also recommended that Byrd's lawyers face ethics charges. Byrd's case had turned into an embarrassment for his many supporters and for the judges of the Sixth Circuit who had believed him. He was executed in February 2002.[33]

The DPIC publishes the most widely cited list of prisoners exonerated and released from death row since 1973. As of this writing (May 2009), the DPIC "Innocence List" was 131 names long. To qualify, a defendant must have persuaded a court to grant him a new trial, resulting either in an acquittal or in the state's dismissing all charges. Also included on the list are those defendants who got an absolute pardon from a governor based on new evidence of innocence.[34]

The DPIC list includes such indisputable miscarriages of justice as the case of Frank Lee Smith, who died on death row from cancer before the DNA test exonerated him. Yet it also includes the somewhat more debatable cases of Kirk Bloodsworth and Ray Krone, which, though they began with a wrongful conviction, did not exactly end as "death row exonerations." Each man had been sentenced to life in prison after winning a new trial.

Surely the fact that someone was acquitted upon retrial is impressive; no one should be convicted of a crime, much less sentenced to death, based on anything less than proof beyond a reasonable doubt. However, acquittal does not always equal "exoneration." Consider a case recently added to the DPIC list, that of Nathson Fields in Illinois. A former "general" in the El Rukns gang, Fields was sentenced to death in 1986 for the 1984 murder of two rival gang members. However, he won a new trial in 1998 when the Illinois Supreme Court ruled that his first trial had been marred by corruption. Ironically, the corruption started with Fields's own lawyer, who offered the judge a $10,000 bribe to acquit Fields. The judge took it, then hastily returned the money and sentenced Fields to death, having gotten wind of a federal investigation in the meantime. A new judge acquitted Fields in April 2009 because he disbelieved the testimony of a key prosecution witness, an admitted murderer. Fields was not really freed "from death row," as the DPIC Web site implies since he had already been granted bond pending his new trial and left prison in 2003.[35]

Another concern is that the DPIC list sometimes blurs the distinction between a prosecutor's decision to drop the charges and proof that the defendant never should have been tried in the first place. For example, the list includes Troy Lee Jones, convicted in California of killing his girlfriend in December 1981; prosecutors believed the motive was to prevent her from telling police Jones had strangled someone else to death 11 months earlier. A neighbor testified that she saw Jones beating the woman with a tire iron a few weeks before she was found shot to death, but police never found a murder weapon. The California Supreme Court granted Jones a new trial in 1996 based on Jones's defense lawyer's failure to attack the prosecution's circumstantial case aggressively enough at the original trial. Prosecutors then dismissed the charges, not because they conceded Jones' innocence but because they could not reconstruct their case after the passage of so much time.[36]

Similarly, Jeremy Sheets was found guilty in 1997 of the racially motivated kidnapping, rape, and murder of a black high school girl 5 years earlier. He left Nebraska's death row in 2001 after the U.S. Supreme Court declined to review a Nebraska Supreme Court decision overturning his conviction. The case against Sheets hinged on a taped confession by his friend and accomplice, Adam Barnett, who turned state's evidence in return for a plea bargain. Barnett recounted how he and Sheets selected their victim out of anger at the white women they knew who had been dating black men. But Barnett committed suicide in jail. The Nebraska high court ruled that the tape should not have been allowed at trial because Sheets's attorney had no opportunity to cross-examine the deceased Barnett. The prosecutor then declined to retry Sheets and dropped the charges. Far from conceding the wrongfulness of Sheets's conviction, the state of Nebraska later refused to return to him a $1,000 contribution he had been required to make to the state's fund for crime victims, citing its belief that he had not been exonerated of the murder.[37]

Such nuances help account for the fact that even Judge Rakoff, though sympathetic to the DPIC's anti-death penalty position, did not accept its findings at face value. Instead, his 2002 ruling striking down the federal death penalty relied on, but did not entirely endorse, the DPIC list. Rakoff conducted his own study of the 58 people whom the DPIC listed as exonerated in the 1993–2001 period. (He chose this interval because it coincided with the time during which the federal statute he was reviewing had been in effect.) This study persuaded the judge that 32 of the men on the list for those years—roughly 55 percent—were "factually innocent" in the sense that they had been definitively cleared by DNA or other means.[38]

The DPIC list overstates the case in another way. It includes 19 men who were set free after 1973, but who were not convicted and sentenced under the law as it now exists during the modern era of capital punishment. Indeed,

5 of the 19 were tried in 1971 or earlier, prior even to *Furman*. Thirteen others were tried during the years between *Furman* and *Gregg*, under state laws that *Gregg* later invalidated. And 2 of the 19 were tried in Ohio prior to the 1978 Supreme Court decision that struck down that state's capital punishment statute because it failed to conform to *Gregg*: it did not allow enough opportunity for defendants to seek leniency in the sentencing phase of a capital trial.[39]

In short, the predicament of these 19 people may confirm the inherent fallibility of any system of justice. But it says nothing about the *current* system's propensity to produce false convictions. If anything, these cases would have been less likely to result in death sentences today thanks to the constitutional safeguards that the Supreme Court created in the 1970s. Indeed, 3 of the 19 cases came from Massachusetts, which got rid of the death penalty in 1974. And two involved men sentenced for crimes—burglary and rape—that are no longer capital offenses today.[40]

So, how many people have been wrongly sentenced to death in the modern era of capital punishment? It is impossible to count with any precision. But it is possible to come up with a reasonable ballpark estimate. From the 131 cases on the DPIC list as of May 2009, we should subtract the 19 cases that went to trial under statutory schemes that no longer exist. That leaves 112 people, including those such as Sheets and Jones, who were hardly "exonerated," as well as others (such as Bloodsworth, Washington, Krone, and Fields) whose death sentences had already been lifted as of the time they were released. To correct for this residual over-inclusiveness, multiply the 112 cases by 55 percent—the validity rate Judge Rakoff found for actual innocence claims for the period from 1993–2001. The judge based his conclusions on unspecified but "conservative" criteria; the rate of innocence he found is therefore a useful proxy for the overall precision of the DPIC list. The result of this admittedly rough exercise would be 62 cases of factual innocence in the post-*Gregg* era.

Is 62 a lot or a little? In a 2002 study, the DPIC's leading critic, California prosecutor Ward A. Campbell, conceded 34 exonerated death row inmates, so it is almost twice that skeptic's estimate number.[41] But it is less than half what the DPIC claimed as of May 2009. And 62 mistaken verdicts would represent eight-tenths of one percent of the 7,280 death sentences meted out by U.S. courts between 1977 and January 1, 2009. In other words, under these assumptions, the criminal justice system got it right 99.2 percent of the time.

ॐॐ

People not only disagree about the death penalty, they disagree passionately. And the intensity of the debate is such that it extends even to the cool confines of the Supreme Court, as the exchange between Justices Souter and Scalia demonstrates. The purpose of this chapter has been not to debunk one side or the other but to inject a sense of perspective. On the issues of race and innocence, a fair reading of the evidence validates neither Scalia-like insouciance nor Souter-like alarm. Plainly, the system is not perfect, but it seems fairer and more accurate than it was before *Gregg*. The mere fact that statisticians have had to hunt for residual racism—and found it only in the form of disparate treatment of white and black victims, not defendants—suggests that something has changed. In the old days, it did not take multivariate regression to find the evidence of racial bias in capital punishment. A similar point could be made about death penalty critics' earnest—but so far futile—search for proof that an innocent man has been executed.

Lingering problems related to race and innocence show that the U.S. death penalty is fallible, but they do not support the notion that it is "broken beyond repair." Rather, the issues appear more contained than the critics suggest, and could probably be further mitigated without abolishing capital punishment. Indeed, to the extent death penalty foes focus on race and innocence, they neglect American capital punishment's truly intractable flaws. It is those deep-rooted problems to which I now turn.

THREE

The Case Against the Case for the Death Penalty

"The cure for the ailments of democracy," the pragmatic philosopher John Dewey wrote, "is more democracy."[1] And for many years after *Gregg*, supporters of capital punishment took a similar view of the death penalty. The dominant impulse, in both legislatures and the courts, was to expand death-eligible crimes and clear procedural obstacles to executing death sentences. Thus in

1989, the Supreme Court issued its ruling in
Teague v. Lane, which curtailed the ability of
death row prisoners to raise constitutional issues through petitions for habeas corpus in
federal court.[2] In 1994, the U.S. Violent Crime
Control and Law Enforcement Act dramatically
expanded the number of federal capital crimes.
In 1996, the Anti-Terrorism and Effective
Death Penalty Act further limited federal
habeas corpus. During the decade beginning
in 1997, five states enacted the death penalty
for rape of a child—though the Supreme Court
struck those laws down in 2008. The court's
ruling showed that the death penalty expan-
sionist wave had, to some extent, crested. Yet
as recently as 2009, Virginia's state legislature
voted to make murder accomplices as well as
actual "triggermen" eligible for the death
penalty. The lawmakers also extended the
death penalty to murderers of auxiliary police
officers and fire marshals, although Governor
Tim Kaine vetoed the bills.[3]

And why not? Certainly one way to ameliorate racial disparities in the death penalty, at
least in theory, would be to sentence more
people to death. If killers of whites are more
likely to face execution than killers of blacks,
simply step up capital prosecutions of the latter. Would more frequent death sentences and

executions increase the risk of executing an innocent person? Perhaps, but that too can be justified. When execution is frequent, swift, and certain, proponents argue, its deterrent effect on murder is strong—the innocent lives saved more than cancel out the innocent lives that might be lost through erroneous executions. "Counterbalancing the concern that even one innocent person may be executed is the question of whether the death penalty saves innocent lives by deterring potential murders," Ward Campbell wrote in 2002.[4] In 2005, two distinguished law professors, Cass Sunstein of the University of Chicago and Adrian Vermeule of Harvard University, suggested that the death penalty might be not only morally permissible but morally mandatory if social scientists could prove that it deterred murder.[5]

There are just two problems. First, people have been debating capital punishment's deterrent effect for centuries and will probably continue to do so forever. Even modern statistical methods are unlikely to produce sufficient certainty on this question. Second, and more fundamentally, the very structure of the criminal justice system in the United States raises substantial obstacles to the death penalty's consistent imposition.

❧❦

In Chapter 1, I argued that the recent decline in the death penalty is likely attributable
to a roughly simultaneous decline in violent
crime, especially homicide. I listed possible
causes for the lower murder rate of the last two
decades, but omitted an obvious candidate:
capital punishment itself. Some supporters of
the death penalty, however, do credit stepped-
up executions for the downward trend in murder. As Dudley Sharp of Justice For All, a
Houston-based pro-death penalty organization, has put it:

> From 1995 to 2000, executions aver-
> aged 71 per year, a 21,000 percent
> increase over the 1966–1980 period.
> The murder rate dropped from a
> high of 10.2 (per 100,000) in 1980 to
> 5.7 in 1999—a 44 percent reduction.
> The murder rate is now at its lowest
> level since 1966.[6]

I agree with law professors Sunstein and
Vermeule: proof of deterrence would certainly
fortify the argument for the death penalty. Indeed, if putting murderers to death definitely

saved innocent lives, it would argue for mandatory execution. At a minimum, it would place organizations such as the Council of Europe, which calls the death penalty an inherently "barbaric" violation of human rights, on the moral defensive. Sunstein and Vermeule point out that states that refused to execute murderers, knowing their inaction would essentially condemn numerous random, innocent people to death, would be as blameworthy as a government that refused to regulate a life-threatening environmental pollutant.

Yet that proof does not exist. The literature on the death penalty and deterrence is vast and highly technical. I do not propose to review it in detail here. Suffice it to say that both sides in the debate start with intuitively plausible claims. On the one hand, the realistic prospect of being caught and executed might cause a potential murderer to think twice about his plans; on the other hand, murderers are quite often not the kind of people who respond rationally to incentives. In recent decades, econometricians have used multivariate regression analysis to show that the rate of execution can explain ups and downs in the homicide rate of various jurisdictions. Such researchers have even suggested precise numbers of lives saved per execution. But they have met with rebuttals

from other social scientists who accuse the
econometricians of cherry-picking data series
or failing to factor in all relevant variables.

In response to Sunstein and Vermeule, Yale
law professor John J. Donohue and Justin
Wolfers, professor of business and public policy at the University of Pennsylvania's Wharton
School, prepared an excellent review of the research on the death penalty and deterrence.[7]
Donohue and Wolfers argue that there is no
way to isolate the impact of executions from
that of other factors that affect homicide rates
because the number of executions historically
has been small and relatively stable compared
to the large and fluctuating number of murders. As they put it:

> The U.S. data simply do not speak
> clearly about whether the death
> penalty has a deterrent or antideter-
> rent effect. The only clear conclusion
> is that execution policy drives little
> of the year-to-year variation in homi-
> cide rates. As to whether executions
> raise or lower the homicide rate, we
> remain profoundly uncertain.[8]

If capital punishment determined the ebb
and flow of homicide over time, that effect

would be evident in comparisons between jurisdictions with and without the death penalty. But Donohue and Wolfers effectively demonstrate that this is not the case with respect to the U.S. and Canada, the latter of which abolished the death penalty in 1967. Homicide rates in the two countries moved in "virtual lockstep" between 1950 and 2004.

Homicide Rates and the Death Penalty in the United States and Canada

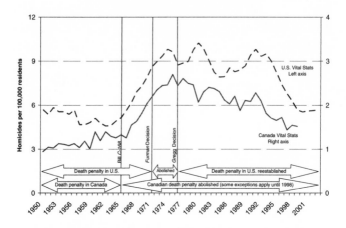

Source: Adapted from "Uses and Abuses of Empirical Evidence in the Death Penalty Debate," by John J. Donohue and Justin Wolfers, *Stanford Law Review*, vol. 58, no. 3 (December, 2005), Figure 2, p. 799.

There is a similar pattern for death penalty and non-death penalty states in the U.S. between 1960 and 2000.

Homicide Rates in the United States

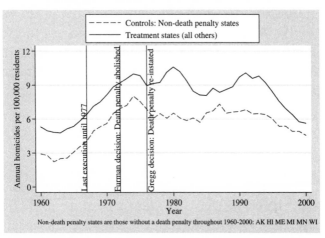

Source: Adapted from "Uses and Abuses of Empirical Evidence in the Death Penalty Debate," by John J. Donohue and Justin Wolfers, *Stanford Law Review*, vol. 58, no. 3 (December, 2005), Figure 3, p. 801.

Given these data, it is hard to disagree with the conclusion of Supreme Court Justice John Paul Stevens: "Despite 30 years of empirical research in the area, there remains no reliable statistical evidence that capital punishment in fact deters potential offenders."[9] To be sure, there is no proof that it does *not* deter them. Having failed to find conclusive answers to the deterrence question after so many years of searching, perhaps both sides in the death penalty debate should simply call off the hunt.

ॐ

I argued in the previous chapter that racial disparities in the U.S. death penalty and the risk of wrongful execution are legitimate issues, but that both have also been overstated by death penalty opponents. Imagine though that neither issue existed at all. For example, suppose that the entire U.S. population consisted of a single racial group and that infallible computers separated the innocent from the guilty, rather than courts and juries. If everything else remained the same, American criminal justice would still produce large and difficult-to-justify discrepancies in the administration of capital punishment.

The first and most obvious reason for this is that criminal justice in the United States is highly decentralized. The federal government in Washington has the power to define and punish certain crimes, but only in areas the Constitution places under its enumerated authority: interstate commerce, say, or the armed forces. For the vast majority of offenses, including the vast majority of homicides, the 50 states retain primary responsibility. Furthermore, within each state, autonomous counties (or, in a few cases, cities) handle criminal investigations and prosecutions. Strictly speaking, there is no "American criminal justice system," but rather 3,141 criminal justice systems—one in each of the counties and "county equivalents" across the country.

Under these circumstances, the federal government can and does pursue a measure of consistency within its limited death penalty purview by channeling the various United States Attorneys' decisions about when and whether to charge federal capital offenses through the Justice Department in Washington. But there is no ready means of harmonizing the capital punishment policies of the states—15 of which do not have the death penalty at all.

Many obvious anomalies arise from this fact alone. In 1992, Jeffrey Dahmer of Milwaukee, Wisconsin was convicted of raping, murdering, and eating 15 men and boys. These monstrous acts would have called for the death penalty if he had committed them just a few dozen miles to the south in Illinois. But, since he killed in a state that abolished capital punishment in 1853, his execution was never even an issue. Someone planning a particularly heinous murder in the suburbs of Washington, D.C., could theoretically eliminate the risk of being executed simply by driving his victim from Maryland or Virginia, which have the death penalty, into the District of Columbia, which does not.

Such differences occur not only *between* death penalty states and non-death penalty states, but also *within* death penalty states. We have already seen that differing political realities and prosecutorial policies in Baltimore County, Maryland and the city of Baltimore next door create a huge divergence between the death-sentencing rate in the majority-white suburb and the majority-black city. This is not an isolated case.

Consider Ohio. Between 1981 and 2002, 8 percent of offenders charged with a capital crime in Cuyahoga County (in which Cleveland is located) received a death sentence at trial, according to a 2005 Associated Press study. Meanwhile, in Hamilton County (home to Cincinnati), 43 percent of those charged with a capital crime wound up on death row. Of Ohio's 88 counties, 12 did not seek the death penalty in a single case between 1981 and 2002, according to the Associated Press.[10]

In Texas, 280 of the 1,014 people sentenced to death in the post-*Gregg* era came from just one of the state's 274 counties, Harris, which Houston dominates. In other words, 28 percent of the death sentences originated in a jurisdiction that contains about 16 percent of the state's total population. By contrast, only 18 offenders—1.8 percent—arrived on death row from El Paso County, which has about 3 percent of the state's total population.[11]

In Washington State, Cecil Emile Davis sits on death row having been convicted of one count of aggravated first degree murder for raping, robbing, suffocating, and poisoning 65-year-old Yoshiko Couch during a 1997 home invasion in Pierce County, home of Tacoma.[12] While undoubtedly heinous, this single murder cannot compare to the record compiled by Gary Ridgway, the notorious "Green River Killer" of next-door King County, where Seattle is located. He admitted raping and murdering

48 women over the course of years in that jurisdiction. Yet in 2003, Ridgway, the worst serial killer in U.S. history, was spared the death penalty and received a sentence of life imprisonment without parole.[13]

To be sure, all of these circumstances have logical explanations. In his study of county-level data within five death penalty states, Theodore Eisenberg of Cornell Law School found that the number of death sentences in a county varies directly with the number of murders in that jurisdiction—just as state death-sentencing rates track state-level homicide figures.[14] Thus, the differences in death-sentencing among Texas counties probably reflect their differing murder rates, according to Eisenberg. He told *The New York Times* that the large number of murders in Harris County explains why it supplies a disproportionate share of the death row inmates in Texas. "Harris County is in the middle of Texas in terms of death sentences," he said. "Harris County is to Texas as Texas is to the nation."[15]

In Ohio, both Cuyahoga County and Hamilton County have white majorities. The Associated Press attributed the difference in their death-sentencing rates to the more conservative politics of Hamilton County, which voted Republican in every presidential election between 1968 and 2004. The experience of Maryland provides some confirmation for this hypothesis. Though Baltimore County votes Democratic, as does most of the state, it is relatively conservative compared to similar jurisdictions elsewhere in Maryland. Baltimore County voted for Democratic presidential candidates at much lower rates than did Montgomery County, a liberal bastion next door to Washington, D.C. (In 2000, for example, Baltimore County gave Al Gore 55 percent of the vote, while Montgomery County gave him 65 percent.) And, since the restoration of capital punishment in Maryland in 1978, prosecutors in Montgomery County have sought the death penalty only one-fifth as often as their counterparts in Baltimore County.[16]

King County prosecutors chose not to pursue the death penalty against Gary Ridgway based on a complicated moral calculation in which the wishes of Ridgway's victims' families weighed unusually heavily. In many cases, the bodies of their loved ones had never been found. They wanted Ridgway to confess to the crimes and show authorities where the victims were buried so they could recover the remains and hold proper funerals. Prosecutors concluded that, on balance, it was worth forgoing the death penalty in return for Ridg-

way's pleading guilty to his crimes and agree-
ing to show police where he had disposed of
his victims.[17]

For some supporters of the death penalty,
intrastate variations in death-sentencing are
not only explicable, but eminently justifiable.
They reflect local democracy in action. District
attorneys are elected. These prosecutors'
charging decisions therefore appropriately reflect the sentiment of the local community—
that is, the people most directly affected by the
crime. Sentencing decisions also reflect the
opinions and needs of local citizens because
juries choose sentences. As a prominent group
of Maryland capital punishment backers wrote
in a recent report, "While jurisdictional differences may exist, it is not illegal or wrong, but
just an example of local government reflecting
the will of the people."[18]

For better or worse, the Constitution recog-
nizes the states' sovereignty with respect to
criminal law and authorizes them to enforce
their differing policy views within their own
boundaries. In a continent-sized country of im-
mense diversity, it may be not only necessary
but in some sense acceptable to accommodate
different regional policies and traditions on the
death penalty. Thus on the Mexican border we
have Texas, and on the Canadian border we

have Michigan, which abolished the death penalty in 1846 and never reinstated it.

Nevertheless, the Constitution also promises equality of treatment under state law, and this guarantee is hard to square with differential treatment of similar crimes within state boundaries. Sometimes local prosecutorial decisions reflect legitimately difficult issues of morality and penology, as when the King County prosecutor chose not to seek death for Gary Ridgway. At other times, they may reflect little more than an individual prosecutor's attitude about capital punishment, his political ambitions, or a particular county's ability to pay the expenses of a capital trial. For example, Ohio counties are now reimbursed by the state for only 31 percent of the cost of providing defense lawyers to capital defendants, which is down from 50 percent a few years ago. The counties allocate widely varying amounts for these legal fees, ranging from $3,000 per case to $75,000.[19]

The net effect is that state law is not applied consistently within a given state. As a result, two people convicted of the same crime could receive different sentences based at least in part on factors that the state legislature never articulated in a statute, and never should: politics, money, race, or some combination of all three. Or their sentences could differ based on no intelligible criteria at all. That may be democracy in action. If so, it simply demonstrates that local democracy can sometimes be at odds with equal justice.

ॐॐ

Federalism—with its decentralized, local control of criminal justice within the states—mainly affects the rate at which offenders get *sentenced* to death. But offenders are not only sentenced inconsistently depending on where they happen to commit their crimes. They are also *executed* at wildly different rates in different places.

Since 1977, the vast majority of U.S. executions have taken place in the states of the South and West, with Texas leading the way. As of January 1, 2009, Texas had carried out 423 of 1,136 post-Gregg executions, or 38 percent of the national total. Texas assembled this record even though it had meted out only 1,014 death sentences, or about 14 percent of the 7,280 during this period. In other words, Texas' share of executions was nearly triple its share of death sentences. Virginia occupies second place, having executed 103 convicted murderers out of 125 sentenced to death since 1977; its share (9 percent) of the national execution total is slightly more than five times its share of death sentences (1.7 percent).[20]

On the other hand, California had condemned 680 men and women (9.3 percent of all post-*Gregg* death sentences), yet it had executed only 13 of them (1 percent of the total number of executions since *Gregg*). Pennsylvania also stands in stark contrast to Texas and Virginia. As of January 1, 2009, there were 224 prisoners on death row in that state, and yet very few of them were executed. Pennsylvania has put just three people to death in the post-*Gregg* era, the last in 1999. All three were "volunteers" who had waived their appeals.[21]

For those put to death in Texas, the average wait time between sentencing and execution was 10.26 years. In Virginia, no executed prisoner waited longer than a decade; in 1998 and 1999, Virginia managed to put eight prisoners to death within 5 years of their sentencing dates. Yet in California, the average time on death row for executed prisoners was nearly 20 years. There have been so few executions in Pennsylvania that no meaningful average wait time can be calculated.[22]

What is going on here? According to much conventional wisdom, the higher rates of execution in Virginia and Texas reflect their violent, vengeful, and racist histories and cultures. Some scholars believe that in these and other Southern states, today's death penalty is a vestige of the harsh, repressive practices of a not-so-distant past. Criminologist Franklin Zimring of the University of California at Berkeley has traced the high rate of executions in Southern states to a "vigilante tradition" rooted in the historical prevalence of lynching there.[23]

Such explanations have some superficial plausibility. It is true that the U.S. states with the longest tradition of death penalty abolition—Maine, Vermont, Michigan, Wisconsin, and Minnesota—are in New England and the Upper Midwest. Meanwhile, Texas had 468 lynchings between 1885 and 1942, and 339 of the victims were black.[24] If any state practiced a racially skewed death penalty in the past, it was Virginia: 201 of the 236 men and women executed in Virginia between 1908 and 1962 were black; and 25 percent of them were put to death for rape or attempted rape. In a 72-hour period during February 1951, Virginia executed seven black men for purportedly raping white women.[25]

But the theory does not stand up to scrutiny. It cannot account for the fact that, between 1930 and 1967, New York had more executions (329) than Texas (297).[26] Nor can it account for the fact that Virginia has carried out the second highest number of post-*Gregg* executions, even though it is tied with North Carolina for the fewest lynchings in any Southern state.[27]

If the South had such a powerful cultural predisposition in favor of the death penalty, this should be evident not only in a greater propensity to execute convicted murderers; it should also result in a greater propensity to sentence them to death. But as the Cornell law professors have demonstrated, between 1977 and 1999 Texas sentenced prisoners to death at a rate of 20 for every 1,000 homicides in the state. This put Texas right in the middle of the death penalty state pack, ahead of Illinois and Washington but behind Ohio and Nebraska, neither of which is in the South and neither of which has an appreciable history of lynching. Indeed, at least through 1999, Texas had a lower propensity to sentence murderers to death than did Pennsylvania, founded by non-violent Quakers; Pennsylvania sent convicts to death row at the rate of 24 per 1,000 murders. Virginia was tied with California at one of the lowest death-sentencing rates of any death penalty state: 13 per 1,000 murders.[28]

A far likelier cause for the differences in execution rates among death penalty states is variance in the policies, procedures, and attitudes of courts around the country. Almost all post-*Gregg* state capital punishment laws include a mandatory appeal to the state supreme court, usually followed by a petition for habeas corpus in the state courts. If denied, each of these proceedings culminates in an appeal—usually also denied—to the Supreme Court of the United States. But at that point, most death row inmates pursue a writ of habeas corpus in the nearest federal district court, followed by an appeal in the U.S. circuit court of appeals, and so on until the Supreme Court of the United States again. The courts sometimes weigh several federal habeas petitions per prisoner.

Only after this entire judicial process—and the possibility of executive clemency—has been exhausted, can state officials finally lead the condemned man (or, far less frequently, the condemned woman) to the death chamber. It takes years, not least because attorneys for a condemned man have every incentive to keep their client alive by pursuing every procedural avenue the law allows. In this sense, even when they lose they win. This frustrates prosecutors, who accuse capital defense lawyers of thwarting the will of the majority through litigation. Yet like federalism, prolonged death penalty cases, both on direct appeal and on state and federal habeas corpus, are a manifestation of the checks and balances built into American government. In this instance, the courts protect against the risk that a state would sentence the wrong man to death—or even that it would condemn the right man through a process that violates his constitutional rights. This is as it should be.

But why should the rate at which the states are able to "convert" death sentences into executions vary so widely? The variations do reflect factors specific to each state, such as differences in rules of procedure. Virginia is notorious among capital defense lawyers for its restrictive appeals process. One Virginia rule bars lawyers from raising any legal objections on appeal that were not brought up during the original trial. Another prevents death row prisoners from having any court consider new evidence discovered more than 21 days after trial; such belated findings can only be presented to the governor in a request for clemency.[29]

Virginia state judges, from the trial courts to the state supreme court, enforce these rules rigorously. This is not surprising, since the ideology of the Virginia state bench reflects the fact that its members have been picked by a state legislature that was dominated by conservatives of both political parties during most of the post-*Gregg* era. In 2000, Professor James S. Liebman of Columbia Law School estimated that the Virginia state courts had reversed only about 13 percent of the death sentences in the state; this was well below the average rate for other states.[30]

Texas picks state court judges, including a seven-member Court of Criminal Appeals that handles death penalty cases, through partisan elections. The system encourages judges to represent—not resist—Texas's pro-death penalty majority. Texas state judges (like those in Virginia) are sticklers for procedural rules, which (like those in Virginia) provide little latitude for death row appeals. A 1995 law set significant time constraints on state habeas corpus petitions, and it limited the number of appeals a defendant can make.[31] A recently published study compared the death penalty appeals process in the 13 federal districts with the most capital habeas corpus cases between 2001 and 2004. According to the study, which was funded by the U.S. Department of Justice, Texas capital appeals moved through the state courts more swiftly than those in any other state in the survey except for Oklahoma. (Virginia was not included in the study.)[32]

Once Virginia and Texas death cases finish their journey through the state courts, they enter the federal courts. In theory, federal law is the same everywhere, so there should be less variation in the results of federal cases. Federal judges are less susceptible to local politics than are state judges because the President appoints them for life. In reality, the selection of lower-court federal judges—both district judges, who are the gatekeepers of federal habeas corpus, and circuit judges, who hear habeas appeals—is highly political. Presidents seek to appoint judges sympathetic to their own party and their own policy views. Therefore, it is not surprising, as Liebman's team of Columbia University researchers noted in a comprehensive 2002 study of capital appeals, that "judges appointed by Republican Presidents are in fact less likely to reverse death verdicts than judges appointed by Democratic Presidents."[33]

Actually, it is even more complicated than that. Because the President's judicial nominees need Senate confirmation, each state's senators leverage their prerogatives under Senate rules to influence the President's choices. Even when a senator is from the op-

posite party, he or she can force the President
to negotiate judicial nominations affecting the
senator's home state or circuit. For most of the
post-*Gregg* era, senators from both Virginia
and Texas have been conservative Republicans
or conservative Democrats. Even during the
relatively liberal presidencies of Democrats
Jimmy Carter and Bill Clinton, therefore,
Texas and Virginia were relatively likely to get
conservative federal judges. This conservative
tendency also prevailed for the federal appeals
courts that review district court rulings from
Virginia and Texas—the U.S. Courts of Appeals
for the Fourth and Fifth Circuits, respectively.

The story in California has been completely
different. After that state reinstated the death
penalty in 1978, a majority of liberal justices
on the California Supreme Court launched
what amounted to a judicial campaign to prevent anyone from actually being executed
under the new law. Between 1979 and 1986,
the court reversed 58 of the 64 death sentences that came to it on appeal. This exasper-
ated California's voters. In 1986, they voted to
recall three of the four justices who had made
up the seven-member court's anti-death
penalty majority: Chief Justice Rose Bird and
Associate Justices Cruz Reynoso and James
Grodin. Subsequent justices got the message.

Since 1986, the California Supreme Court has affirmed 90 percent of death sentences.[34]

In April 1992, California readied its first execution in 25 years: that of Robert Alton Harris, who had been convicted of kidnapping two teenage boys and shooting them to death. The stakes were high: both opponents and supporters of capital punishment in California sensed that if Harris's execution took place, it would help usher in a new era of executions in the nation's largest state. Harris's guilt was not in question, but there was evidence he was a victim of horrific child abuse. Then-Governor Pete Wilson, a Republican, publicly agonized before denying Harris executive clemency: "As great as is my compassion for Robert Harris the child," Wilson said, "I cannot excuse or forgive the choice made by Robert Harris the man."[35]

But judicial resistance to California's death penalty was not over. It had simply shifted from the state supreme court justices to the judges of the state's federal district courts and the San Francisco-based U.S. Court of Appeals for the Ninth Circuit, which had several members appointed by President Carter, and many who were appointed under the strong influence of Democratic senators from California during the post-*Gregg* period. As Harris's execution time approached, individual district judges

and members of the Ninth Circuit issued a series of orders staying Harris's execution, citing
the need to hear Harris's new claims including
his contention that California's use of lethal
gas as a means of execution would be cruel
and unusual punishment. The last of these
stays came after Harris had already been
strapped into the gas chamber. The Supreme
Court of the United States, then headed by
Chief Justice William H. Rehnquist—an ap-
pointee of President Richard Nixon and
staunch supporter of the death penalty—
slapped down each stay in turn. The Supreme
Court finally told California to ignore any order
to delay Harris's execution that did not em-
anate from the high court itself. [36]

The chaotic Harris case helped fuel a legislative movement to limit death row appeals,
which culminated in the limitations on federal
habeas corpus enacted by Congress as part of
the 1996 Anti-Terrorism and Effective Death
Penalty Act. But, due to an infusion of judges
appointed by President Clinton and the continuing influence of Democratic senators, the federal courts on the West Coast still treat death
penalty appeals sympathetically. The federal
district courts in California grant three-quar-
ters of capital habeas corpus petitioners time
to pursue claims in state court that they failed

to pursue earlier. This step, which is far less common in Texas and Virginia, adds an average of 2 years to each case.[37] Consequently, the average California death row habeas case takes 6.2 years to get through federal district court. Appeals in the Ninth Circuit take more than 4 years each on average. Between 1978 and 2007, federal courts granted some form of relief to California death row inmates in 70 percent of cases.[38]

Data for Pennsylvania are scarcer than for California, but the available figures suggest that the performance of the federal judiciary may help explain the slow pace of executions in that state as well. Roughly half of the people sentenced to death in Pennsylvania were prosecuted in Philadelphia. But the Philadelphia-area district court took more time to finish habeas corpus petitions than any of its counterparts in the 13 busiest districts—except for the California district courts and one Ohio court. Like California's federal district judges, Philadelphia's frequently gave petitioners stays of execution so they could file claims in state court, and those stays lasted longer than any other court's.[39] This caused the elected chief justice of the Pennsylvania Supreme Court to complain in a 2008 opinion that the federal court was allowing death row inmates "to ignore Pennsylvania state court procedural defaults in capital cases."[40] Once the Philadelphia-area federal district court finally ruled, it granted death row prisoners relief 75 percent of the time.[41]

❦

For death row inmates and their lawyers, the fact that different death penalty states have different laws and procedures for capital appeals can seem more or less advantageous, more or less frustrating—even more or less fair. Ideally, each death penalty state would have an identical approach in order to eliminate discrepancies in the treatment of capital cases across the country. However, the federal structure in the U.S. makes such uniformity rather improbable. The state is the level of government responsible for criminal law enforcement, and therefore the most important thing is that each state's rules be applied consistently throughout its jurisdiction.

But differences among execution rates based on varying interpretations of federal law by federal courts are problematic. The federal judiciary exists to secure the rights that each U.S. citizen enjoys under the Constitution and the laws enacted by Congress. These are supposed to be the same for everyone, everywhere, regardless of state boundaries. To be sure, the Supreme Court of the United States can correct the most egregious errors of the individual circuits and resolve conflicts among them. But this takes time and, in the meantime, the high court cannot stop the myriad lower courts from pursuing differing interpretations of the law—or, in some cases, their various policy agendas regarding capital punishment. Intended to check and balance the states' unconstitutionally idiosyncratic practices or procedures, federal judicial regulation of capital punishment has instead evolved into yet another source of contradiction and confusion.

FOUR

A Special Penalty for Special Cases

In *Gregg v. Georgia*, the U.S. Supreme Court tried to create a rational death penalty for the nation within two constraints. The first constraint was the justices' awareness that capital punishment cried out for reform because it was historically marred by systematic racism and other arbitrary state and local considerations. The second constraint was their acknowledgment that public opinion favored the death penalty and made the court's solution in *Furman*—de facto abolition—unstable. *Gregg* represented the court's attempt to retreat from *Furman* without retreating from the principle enshrined in *Furman*: that state and local majorities should apply the death penalty more equitably and more accurately and should reserve it for only those criminals identified by Americans through their legislators as the worst of the worst.

To an underappreciated extent, the court's *Gregg* compromise achieved its aims. Whatever residual racism remains in the death penalty today is inexcusable, but is far less dramatic than the discrimination that pervaded capital punishment prior to *Furman*—and less dramatic than contemporary death penalty critics claim. The post-*Gregg* death penalty system still risks a wrongful execution; but this risk, while uncomfortably real, is probably smaller than critics claim and has not yet verifiably materialized. Moreover, the recent decline in death sentences reduces the risk of a wrongful execution; as fewer people are sentenced to death, the chance that an innocent person will die diminishes.

In other crucial ways, however, the court's compromise has failed. In *Gregg*, the court tried to fix the system mainly by changing the jury's decision-making process. By requiring states to specify death-eligibility criteria and to split capital trials into guilt and penalty phases, the court narrowed the universe of capital crimes and forced greater attention to each individual defendant's culpability. But it did nothing about the power of county prosecutors to choose cases from within that universe. And by fostering mandatory state court appeals, as well as creating grounds for new appeals in the federal courts, *Gregg*—and subsequent Supreme Court case law based on it—both added to delays in execution and subjected those delays to the regional and ideological vagaries of judicial decision-making.

Unlike race or innocence, the twin issues of variable prosecutorial discretion and variable jurisprudence loom larger as the death penalty gets smaller. The decline in the death penalty has come about neither because of any fundamental shift in public opinion on capital punishment nor because of a conscious legislative effort to redesign it. It has declined mostly due to a welcome but unplanned phenomenon: a steep drop in murder. The post-*Gregg* patchwork of federal, state, and local rules, standards, and criteria remains mostly intact. Therefore, as the number of executions declines, it becomes more difficult to explain why one of them should occur rather than another. Each increasingly resembles the "lightning strike" that the court denounced in *Furman*.

In short, the full realization of *Gregg*'s goals remains to be accomplished. The decline of the death penalty creates an opportunity to finish the task: to create a death penalty that targets "the worst of the worst," and only them, more consistently than the current system. But we have not yet seized this opportunity. The time has come to shrink the death penalty deliberately, as a matter of policy, according to criteria that reflect the lessons of the post-*Gregg* era. We need to radically rethink eligibility for capital punishment. The death penalty should no longer be thought of as an instrument of ordinary law enforcement, but as a truly special penalty for truly special cases.

৵৵

To be sure, the only way to guarantee an end to all the contradictions and difficulties of the death penalty is to abolish it. That, of course, is the position of the anti-capital punishment movement. The argument that the death penalty is "broken beyond repair" has been embraced recently not only by the state legislatures of New Jersey and New Mexico but also by the majority of a blue-ribbon state commission in Maryland, which surveyed alleged jurisdictional and racial disparities in its capital punishment system and concluded that the death penalty should be abolished because "no procedural or administrative changes . . . would eliminate" the disparities.[1] Maryland nevertheless retained the death penalty, albeit in a highly restricted form that required biological evidence or video evidence to support a capital conviction.[2]

Yet death penalty abolitionists would oppose even a perfectly consistent death penalty. Death penalty abolitionism in its purest form is, like pacifism, a principled position. Those who adhere to it do so out of moral conviction and without concern for the consequences of eliminating the death penalty. Like all such principled stands, it is worthy of respect. And, admittedly, the case for abolishing capital punishment is stronger if one assumes, as I do, that there is no way to know whether the death penalty deters murder.

Furthermore, death penalty opponents are right to argue that no one should be put to death if an adequate alternative punishment exists—they suggest life in prison without parole—just as war should only be embarked upon as a last resort. The death penalty should be used if and only if it serves a purpose that no other punishment can.

There are, however, two such purposes. The first is appropriate retribution: some crimes are so horrible that the only punishment that fits is the physical elimination of the perpetrator. Retribution remains one of the few purposes of capital punishment whose constitutionality has been specifically and repeatedly acknowledged by a majority of the Supreme Court. And though it has fallen out of favor with modern liberals, especially those in Europe who emphasize capital punishment's inherent injury to human dignity, retribution actually has deep roots in Western humanitarian thought. No less a liberal than the German philosopher Immanuel Kant argued that the death penalty affirmed human dignity, both that of the murder victim and that of the perpetrator, since it paid due respect to the latter's free will. For Kant, if an offender "has committed murder, he must die. In this case, no possible substitute can satisfy justice. For there is no parallel between death and even the most miserable life, so that there is no equality of crime and retribution unless the perpetrator is judicially put to death."[3]

Of course, Kant's proposition cannot be proven in a mathematical sense, just as the moral reasoning of capital punishment's abolitionists—including Kant's contemporary, the Italian lawyer Cesare Beccaria, against whom the German philosopher aimed his arguments—cannot be proven. Still, Kant was giving philosophical voice to one of humanity's oldest and most persistent moral intuitions. That intuition lies at the root of American public opinion, which remains stubbornly pro-death penalty even after capital punishment's abolition in Europe.

Nor is this a merely American or even Western attitude. Japan still practices the death penalty and, in contrast to the United States, has been employing it *more* frequently in recent years.[4] Capital punishment is highly popular in that country, according to opinion polls. Faced with criticism from abroad, the Japanese government has offered a neo-Kantian rationale for its policy. In 2008, the Japanese Justice Minister Kunio Hatoyama explained to a visiting delegation of European Union diplomats that his society "places extreme importance on the sanctity of life. For that very reason, we feel extreme anger toward those who rob another of life. We have a culture of repaying a death with a death. I feel proud to have been born into such a culture. I feel that, on the contrary, giving someone life in prison rather than the death penalty no matter how many people they kill is a dry and coldly logical way of thinking."[5]

The second objective that execution uniquely can achieve is absolute and final incapacitation of a particular perpetrator. This is, perhaps, a less pressing concern in the United States today where, for the first time in the nation's history, most states and the federal government permit a sentence of life in prison without the chance of release and have the means to carry it out. Nevertheless, life without parole cannot eliminate the risk that the offender could issue instructions to confederates or followers outside prison, escape, persuade an executive authority to grant him clemency, or win a judicial ruling in favor of his release.

Critics of capital punishment are properly sensitive to the remote but real risk of a wrongful capital conviction; but the small chance of a wrongful release from a life-without-parole sentence would seem worthy of their concern as well. This is especially true for extremely violent and willful offenders whose return to society is likeliest to put innocent lives at risk.*

How then to decide when it is necessary and appropriate to punish with death? If the

---

* As this book was going to press, information emerged underscoring the relevance of both perspectives. *The New Yorker* mag-

hardest question for death penalty proponents
is what to do about the risk of wrongful execu-

azine published an article arguing that Cameron Todd Willingham, executed by Texas in 2004 for the arson-murder of his
three children in Corsicana, Texas, might have been wrongfully
convicted. According to the article, experts versed in the latest
forensic techniques believe the fire that killed Willingham's children might well have been accidental, and not deliberately set
as the official investigation concluded. An arson expert echoed
that conclusion in a report to the Texas Forensic Science Commission whereupon Governor Rick Perry, who had presided over
Willingham's execution and was running for re-election, reshuf-
fled the commission's personnel and significantly delayed its
consideration of the case. Meanwhile, local officials and residents of Corsicana defended the Willingham prosecution. Willingham's former wife, the mother of the three dead children,
issued an open letter in which she strongly defended the verdict
and death sentence. Her statement recounted a death row con-
versation in which, she says, Willingham privately conceded his
guilt in an unsuccessful effort to win her support for his
clemency plea. At this stage, it is unclear whether the Willingham case will prove to be the anti-death penalty movement's
long-sought example of an actual wrongful execution in the
post-Gregg era, or a repeat of the Roger Coleman and John Byrd
debacles. See David Grann, "Trial By Fire," *The New Yorker*,
September 7, 2009, pp. 42-63; Janet Jacobs, "No Doubts," *Corsicana Daily Sun*, September 7, 2009, http://www.corsicanadai-
lysun.com/thewillinghamfiles/local_story_250180658.html;
"Stacy Kuykendall's statement about the 1991 fire," http://
www.rickperry.org/media-articles/stacy-kuykendalls-
statement-about-1991-fire. Meanwhile, police in Northern California discovered kidnap victim Jaycee Lee Dugard alive 18
years after she was abducted on her way to elementary school
near Lake Tahoe. The alleged kidnapper, Phillip Garrido, was a
convicted kidnapper and rapist who was released on parole in
1988 after serving 11 years of concurrent federal and Nevada
state sentences of 50 years and life in prison. Garrido held
Dugard as a sex slave. Police see him as a possible suspect in a
string of unsolved murders of girls and women near his Antioch,
California, home. See Jaxon Van Derbeken, Kevin Fagan, Wyatt
Buchanan, and Carolyn Jones, "Search for ties to '90s killings,"
San Francisco Chronicle, August 29, 2009, p. A1.

tion, then the hardest question for death penalty abolitionists is what they would have done with the Nazi leaders condemned to death at Nuremberg. These men were guilty not only of the most horrible mass murder imaginable; they were also the fanatical nucleus of a political movement. Alive, even behind bars, they could have served as a rallying point for unrepentant Nazis or helped to resurrect that movement. That is one lesson of Adolf Hitler's own career. Convicted of high treason after his failed putsch in Munich in 1923, Hitler was sentenced only to prison, wrote *Mein Kampf* in his cell, won early release, and went on to found the Third Reich.

In our own time, Serbia's former ruler Slobodan Milosevic faced 66 counts of crimes against humanity and violations of the laws of war, 1 count of genocide, and 1 count of complicity in genocide for the massacre of 7,000 Muslim men and boys at Srebrenica, Bosnia in 1993. For these unspeakable crimes, however, the maximum penalty he faced from the International Tribunal for the Former Yugoslavia was life in prison. (Milosevic ended up dying in detention during his trial.) The Rome Statute of the International Criminal Court stipulates that the maximum penalty for war crimes, crimes against humanity, and genocide should be life in prison—with possible release after 25 years.[6]

These rules would astonish Kant. I certainly find them a bit surreal. There is such a vast disproportion between a verdict of guilty for murdering thousands and a sentence that not only lets the perpetrator live but also potentially to return to society some day. To be sure, omission of the death penalty in international tribunals reflects the influence of the European Union countries that helped establish them. But, on the death penalty for war criminals, the policy of Europe's governments may not correspond to the moral sentiments of Europeans. In 2006, according to the Novatris/Harris survey, 69 percent of British respondents favored executing another mass murderer, Saddam Hussein, as did 58 percent of French respondents, 53 percent of Germans, and 51 percent of Spaniards. A poll sponsored by the German magazine *Stern* found that 50 percent of Germans favored Saddam's execution and only 39 percent opposed it.[7]

A similar argument applies to authors of mass terrorism, such as Osama bin Laden and Timothy McVeigh, the Oklahoma City bomber who killed 168 people including 19 children. Like the leaders of murderous governments, the leaders of murderous political movements are not only guilty of particularly horrific crimes but are also capable of posing continuing dangers even if incarcerated.

Certainly, execution could convert terrorists into martyrs, inflame their followers, and lead to more violence. But imprisonment does not necessarily eliminate that risk. Consider West Germany's conflict with the terrorist Red Army Faction (RAF) during the 1970s. Four leaders were sentenced to life imprisonment in April 1977 and incarcerated in a maximum security prison. Their followers, communicating with them via coded messages smuggled in and out by defense lawyers, retaliated in July by kidnapping the president of the West German Employers' Association. The kidnappers killed three police officers and a chauffeur in the attack, and then demanded the RAF leaders' release in return for their hostage. When the Bonn government demurred, Arab terrorists with RAF ties seized a Lufthansa flight; they too demanded freedom for the RAF. The terrorists killed the plane's captain. A West German anti-terrorist team stormed the plane and killed three of the four hijackers, freeing the passengers. Hearing the news, three of the RAF prisoners committed suicide in prison; a fourth attempted suicide but survived. The bloody "German Autumn" culminated on October 19 when police in France found the RAF's hostage, murdered by his kidnappers, in the trunk of a car. Perhaps not surprisingly, 1977 saw a surge in support for the death penalty among the West German public.[8]

Genocidaires and terrorists occupy the top level of a death-deserving hierarchy whose next levels should probably be reserved for serial killers such as Jeffrey Dahmer or those who murder multiple victims in a single criminal act. Depraved individual killings—premeditated murders involving torture, murders of small children, sadistic rape-murders and other deeds that "shock the conscience," to use a time-honored legal phrase—also belong on the death-eligible list. And in 28 of the 35 death penalty states, capital offenses include murders that are, in the boilerplate of the statutes, "especially heinous, atrocious, cruel, or depraved (or involved torture)."

Admittedly, this category may be hard to define. The example I would offer of a single murder that should definitely qualify is Austrian Josef Fritzl's murder of his newborn son. Fritzl imprisoned his own daughter for 24 years in a sound-proof basement, repeatedly raping her and conceiving seven children that she delivered, alone, in that dungeon. One of these incestuously-conceived babies experienced respiratory distress at birth in the cellar; Fritzl callously refused to get help and then threw the lifeless infant into an incinerator. (Convicted in 2008 for these monstrous deeds, Fritzl received the maximum penalty allowable under Austrian law: life in a facility for the criminally insane, with a chance for release after 15 years.)

The first goal of death penalty reform in the United States would be to rewrite existing capital laws to restrict the penalty only to criminals whose deeds are most closely comparable to those of Milosevic, the RAF, Dahmer, and Fritzl. To do so, the U.S. could look to an important 1983 ruling by the Supreme Court of Japan that has guided capital prosecutions in that country. The court said capital punishment should be reserved for cases in which it is warranted by the "persistency and brutality of the act of killing," "the number of murder victims," and "the effect on society" of the crime.[9]

This would have different implications for federal and state law. The U.S. government already has primary responsibility for war crimes and terrorism, which is as it should be since these offenses are by nature usually directed at the country as a whole, and often occur on federal property or in federal buildings—or in the field of foreign relations where federal authority is paramount. Yet existing federal death penalty law seeks to punish a range of offenses well beyond these. The 1988 Anti-Drug Abuse Act and the 1994 Violent Crime Control and Law Enforcement Act, passed in election years at a time of mounting public demand for the death penalty, expanded the list of federal capital crimes. There are now 47 such crimes, including: illegal migrant smuggling resulting in death; obstruction of free exercise of religious rights resulting in death; and murder with a firearm in the course of committing a federal violent crime or drug crime. The federal list should be pared to reflect Congress's uniquely national responsibility for defending against large-scale terrorist attacks or crimes against humanity.

As before, the vast majority of capital crimes would be punishable by the states. But their laws must focus much more sharply on the "worst of the worst." Probably the most important step would be to eliminate the death penalty for single murders committed in the course of another common felony, such as kidnapping, robbery, and arson. Some 22 of 35 death penalty states currently make such "felony murders" capital, including most of the states with the largest death rows and largest numbers of executions.[10] As a result, "felony murders" account for a large percentage of death sentences around the United States. For example, in California 87 percent of all first-degree murders are potential capital cases, mostly because of the felony murder provision. And 302 of the 670 inmates on California's death row as of mid-2008 were there on felony murder convictions.[11]

A common felony murder scenario is a killing in the course of burglary or robbery, such as convenience store shootings. While undoubtedly deeply tragic, especially for surviving family members, such crimes do not shock the conscience in the same way that deliberate mass killings or torture-murders do (particularly if rape is defined as a form of torture). They are "ordinary" crimes. They do not cry out unmistakably for retribution. Those who commit them are less likely to be as utterly dangerous and irredeemable as a man like Josef Fritzl plainly is after 24 years of kidnapping, rape, and murder.

Several groups have proposed narrowing the death penalty in this way—to eliminate capital punishment for felony murder, but retain it for a few especially monstrous crimes, such as multiple murders and torture-murders. The Illinois Governor's Commission on

Capital Punishment, the California Commission on the Fair Administration of Justice, and a blue ribbon commission assembled by the Constitution Project (a Washington-based non-profit civil liberties organization) have suggested such reforms. Among the potential benefits, especially if reforms were adopted by all death penalty states, would be greater uniformity in the death penalty's application in different counties, and the freeing up of resources for capital trials and appeals.

It is also possible that the elimination of felony murder as a capital offense would help ameliorate lingering racial disparities in the death penalty. An analysis by sociologist Scott Phillips of the University of Denver suggests that capital punishment for robbery-murder, a typical form of felony murder, may disproportionately affect black defendants in certain jurisdictions. Phillips found that, of capital crimes committed between 1992 and 1999 by black defendants in Harris County, Texas, robbery-murders were the most common, accounting for 79 percent of cases. Robbery murders made up only 61 percent of capital cases against white defendants.[12]

Reconfiguring the death penalty as a special penalty for special crimes would restore a certain moral clarity to capital punishment.

But by itself this step would not do enough to reduce the jurisdictional and other imbalances that still plague the death penalty. A monster like Gary Ridgway might still bargain his way out of a death sentence while another lesser killer in the same state could be sentenced to death. The way to address such discrepancies is to reduce or, preferably, eliminate local prosecutors' power to decide who is charged with a capital crime and who is not. That choice should instead be centralized in a single state agency responsible for ensuring a measure of consistency and proportionality—as the U.S. Attorney General's Review Committee on Capital Cases currently assesses potential federal death cases facing each of the various United States Attorneys around the country.

Prominent figures have suggested such reforms, including former Maryland Governor Parris Glendening and the Illinois commission on capital punishment, but they made little headway politically.[13] The reason is, alas, obvious: local prosecutors cling jealously to their power over the death penalty. Prosecutors argue, in good faith, that their autonomy concerning the death penalty helps ensure that their policy reflects their constituents' will. Of course, it is also true that prosecutors like having the death penalty as an issue they can ride to re-election or higher office, either by supporting it or opposing it.

Ironically, by insisting on their autonomy, prosecutors may be putting the death penalty generally at risk. The Gary Ridgway case illustrates the point. No sooner had King County prosecutors cut their deal to give the serial killer a life sentence than lawyers for other men on Washington State's death row filed suit on behalf of their clients, demanding that they too be spared execution. If Ridgway did not deserve death, they argued, no one does. The Washington State death penalty survived by the narrowest of margins: a 5–4 ruling by the state supreme court in 2006. The majority opinion simply called the Ridgway case a "horrific aberration," and the plea deal that spared him execution "highly rational." But the dissent noted that "when Gary Ridgway, the worst mass murderer in this state's history, escapes the death penalty, serious flaws become apparent." [14]

To be sure, the states are under no constitutional obligation to ensure the comparative proportionality of the death sentences within their borders. In 1984, the Supreme Court of the United States ruled that the Eighth Amendment does not require states to make sure they treat all capital cases similarly.[15]

Still, 19 death penalty states have laws requiring their courts to conduct some sort of "proportionality review," and 2 other states, Florida and Arkansas, do so as a matter of state supreme court precedent.[16]

As the Ridgway case illustrated, this *post hoc* judicial review is deeply problematic. It effectively requires judges to second-guess not only jury verdicts but prosecutorial charging decisions. The criteria can never be entirely clear: should courts compare all cases in which a death sentence actually resulted? Or the much larger group of cases in which a death sentence might have resulted? Examining the literature on state court proportionality review, scholar Timothy V. Kaufman-Osborn concluded that "empirical assessments of the conduct of proportionality review in the states that have retained such review have been mixed at best."[17]

Far better to have the executive authorities of a state scrub the caseload for consistency in advance. Along with that responsibility, the state government should also assume the costs of prosecuting the capital cases it selects. This would eliminate another source of disparities in the existing system: the inability of poorer, rural counties to pay for death penalty trials they might otherwise have pursued.

None of these reforms would directly affect the variation in approaches to death penalty cases by the federal district courts and courts of appeals. There probably is not much that could be done about this short of legislation to alter the courts' habeas corpus jurisdiction. And even that might not make much difference. Congress attempted to rein in anti-death penalty judges through the 1996 Anti-Terrorism and Effective Death Penalty Act (AEDPA), which imposed tighter deadlines on habeas corpus petitions and limited the power of federal judges to second-guess state court denials of habeas. Nevertheless, the average stay on death row has continued to lengthen, in part because judges and defense lawyers have found ways around the AEDPA limitations.[18]

But the reforms I have suggested here might at least indirectly ameliorate this issue. If capital punishment in general were more clearly aimed at "the worst of the worst," and if it were more centrally and consistently applied within states, individual sentences would probably be that much less vulnerable to challenges in federal court. Certainly a more focused death penalty would be less vulnerable to claims that it is biased according to the race of the victim, or that it sweeps up so many defendants that some of them are bound to be innocent.

❧❧

Americans demand a lot from the death penalty. They want it to strike those who most deserve it, but only those who most deserve it. They want execution to follow swiftly after sentencing, but they also want defendants to get due process, as the Constitution guarantees. To be sure, not all Americans want these often competing outcomes in equal measure. The majority would probably favor a death penalty that applies to more killers with fewer opportunities for appeal, while a minority favors the opposite, and an even smaller but influential minority favors outright abolition.

Our decentralized political and legal system enshrines the majority will in black-letter laws, but also enables the minority to have an impact on the actual carrying out of those laws, largely through litigation or the threat thereof. The majority must accept this, in order to retain the death penalty at all. U.S. Court of Appeals Judge Alex Kozinski alluded to this unsatisfactory but inescapable compromise when he wrote in 1995 that "the Supreme Court's death penalty case law reflects an uneasy accommodation between the will of the popular majority, who favor capital punishment, and the objections of a much smaller—but ferociously committed—minority, who view it as a barbaric anachronism."[19]

The result is a capital punishment system that purports to satisfy everyone but does not fully satisfy anyone—and costs a lot of money to operate. A major reason that appeals in California capital cases drag on so long is the state's inability (or refusal) to pay lawyers sufficiently attractive fees to handle death row cases. A chief justice of the state's supreme court has estimated that it can take 3 or 4 years just to find a qualified lawyer willing to represent a death row inmate in his mandatory state appeal at the rates California pays.[20] But these and other budgetary problems are symptoms, not causes, of the deeper contradictions or ambivalence within the public's attitude toward the death penalty.

In 1977, *Gregg* implied that the states could operate even relatively large-scale death penalties in an equitable and consistent manner, as long as they properly channeled jury discretion. But experience since that landmark case has taught a different lesson, as Kozinski also recognized. "Increasing the number of crimes punishable by death, widening the circumstances under which death may be imposed, obtaining more guilty verdicts and expanding death row populations," he wrote, "will do nothing to insure that the very worst members of our society are put to death."[21] When it comes to capital punishment and fundamental fairness, the Zen masters' wisdom might apply: less is more.

The question then is who should refine the death penalty. One option is to continue to rely on the Supreme Court. As an arbiter of capital punishment's parameters, the Court does offer certain advantages. The justices are insulated both in theory and to a considerable degree in reality from politics. Not only that, through judicial review they can trump majoritarian politics. And, of course, it is precisely politics—federal, state and local—that has so often stood in the way of sensible death penalty reform. The capital punishment debate is too often dominated at the legislative level by extremes, pro and con, making the court that much more attractive as a Solomonic alternative.

Reviewing state capital punishment laws under the Eighth Amendment, the court has abolished the death penalty for juvenile offenders, the mentally retarded, and those accused of raping children. In each case, the court rested its decision on its assessment that a "national consensus" had formed to support those changes. The court relied on the fact that a number of state legislatures and juries had turned against capital punishment for juveniles, the mentally retarded, and child rapists—the same rationale it relied on in striking down the death penalty for adult rape in the 1977 case of *Coker v. Georgia.* In each ruling, the court maintained that the Constitution empowered it to exercise its own "independent judgment" in deciding the proportionality of sentences under the Eighth Amendment as well.

And with respect to juveniles and the mentally retarded, the court's rulings have passed the test of public acceptance. The justices seem to have exercised their judgment in a way that felicitously both spared legislators the trouble of dealing with these politically fraught subjects and gave most of their constituents what they wanted. Polls showed that executing the mentally retarded and juvenile offenders were, in principle, highly unpopular with the voters. In short, the court was stretching the limits of its strictly judicial role—it was making policy—but with little risk of triggering a backlash like the one that greeted *Furman.*

But popular as those decisions might have been, the court pushes the boundaries of its own legitimacy and of basic norms of demo-

cratic accountability when it undertakes to decide such issues. The court's method of determining national consensus—essentially con-
ducting a head count of state statutes—is
deeply problematic. Perhaps it made sense in
Coker; in that case, every state but one lacked
the death penalty for rape of an adult, and
most of the states that previously did authorize
it had chosen to abandon it upon rewriting
their capital statutes post-*Furman*. In the
cases of the mentally retarded and juveniles,
however, the majority of non-death penalty
states the court identified was much smaller
than the majority of non-capital rape states in
Coker. As dissenting justices in both cases
pointed out, the head count approach begged
obvious questions: In determining national
consensus, why should heavily populated
states be weighted equally with lightly populated states? Why should possibly transitory
state majorities be accorded finality for Constitutional purposes? Where did the court find
authority in the Constitutional text for the exercise of "independent judgment?" Even more
controversially, the court attempted to bolster
its opinions with allusions to public opinion
polls and foreign legal authorities.

The court's approach reached a kind of
breaking point in 2008 when it struck down

Louisiana's death penalty for child rape, along with similar statutes in five other states. In that case, *Kennedy v. Louisiana*, the court performed its usual head count, noting that only a tiny handful of states imposed death for this heinous but non-lethal crime. But it had to brush aside the fact that the number of states with the death penalty for child rape was increasing rapidly. This contradicted the court's reasoning in *Atkins* and *Roper*, which relied on the fact that a shrinking number of states had retained the death penalty for the mentally retarded and juveniles, respectively. As Justice Samuel A. Alito noted in dissent in *Kennedy*, the court's argument was also based on skewed assumptions, since legislative activity in the states had been affected by confusion over whether *Coker* also made the death penalty for the rape of a child unconstitutional.[22]

Perhaps most embarrassing for the court, however, another factual predicate of its holding—that the federal government did not authorize the death penalty for child rape—turned out to be false. Though neither the justices nor the parties mentioned it during the pendency of the case, in 2006 Congress had actually enacted a statute providing for the execution of members of the armed services found guilty of raping children. The statute had passed by a huge bipartisan majority in the House of Representatives and a 95–0 vote in the Senate. This was hardly surprising since polls showed that a large majority of the public believed those who rape small children should be put to death. Nevertheless, the court denied a petition for rehearing by the state of Louisiana and its ruling stood.[23]

This is not to say that the court was wrong, as a matter of policy. Whether non-lethal crimes—even extremely odious ones like the rape of a small child—can ever count among the "worst of the worst" deserving of the death penalty is a very close question. Pedophiles have a notoriously high recidivism rate, which argues for putting them to death as a guarantee against their committing further crimes. Yet the court was right to worry about re-capitalizing the crime of rape, no matter what the victim's age, given this country's history of racially-tinged sex crime prosecutions. The court was also right to worry that making child rape punishable by death could backfire by giving assailants an additional incentive to intimidate their victims into silence.

Even so, *Kennedy* exploded the mystique of the court's "independent judgment." The justices' ability to wade through the difficult policy issues was manifestly no greater and, in some senses, possibly less than that of the state legislatures whose decision-making the court had pre-empted. It is doubtful that a legislature, open to the views and information of the entire public, not just the litigants and court-approved amicus curiae, would have missed a fact as important and obvious as the existence of a relevant federal statute. If it had made such an error, it could have revisited the matter without risking much collateral damage to its institutional legitimacy. In contrast, the justices' opinion failed the test of logic and, more to the point, factuality: it simply is not true that there is a "national consensus" against executing child rapists.

The lesson of *Kennedy*—like *Furman* before it—is that there is a price to be paid for counting on the Supreme Court to settle the hard questions concerning the death penalty. That price is measured in the coin of judicial legitimacy, a value as vital, in its way, to our constitutional system as the values protected by the Eighth Amendment. With *Kennedy*, the court may have reached a tipping point beyond which it is no longer quite so safe to embark on major death penalty refinements. Further changes—much less outright judicial abolition—would entail more raw assertions of judicial power.

The court has probably substituted for democratic deliberation as much as it should and can. The time has come for the people and their elected representatives, both in state legislatures and Congress, to retake the initiative. The question posed by the death penalty's decline is not only what the right number of executions is: more, fewer, the same amount, or none. It is whether a democratic political system like that of the United States can make such decisions in a way that both serves legitimate goals of public policy and commands the respect of fair-minded people at home and abroad.

ACKNOWLEDGEMENTS

Many people deserve my thanks for their help in making this book possible. Foremost among them are Peter Berkowitz and Tod Lindberg of the Hoover Institution, who encouraged me to write it and provided crucial institutional support, as well as thoughtful critiques of the manuscript. I also benefitted from wise comments offered by Professor Douglas A. Berman of the Ohio State University's Moritz College of Law and Benjamin Wittes of the Brookings Institution. Peter, Tod, Doug, and Ben are wonderful students of the law and public policy, as well as friends from whom I have learned much over the years. But none of them agrees with everything in this book; all are completely blameless for any errors it may contain.

Other researchers who graciously shared their expertise include Professor Theodore Eisenberg of Cornell University Law School, Professor Scott Phillips of the University of Denver, Professor Nancy King of Vanderbilt Law School, Kent Scheidegger of the Criminal Justice Legal Foundation, Professor William J. Bowers of the State University of New York at Albany's Capital Jury Project, Professor James Alan Fox of Northeastern University, and Professor Christian Boulanger of the Humboldt University in Berlin, Germany. Professor William J. Stuntz of the Harvard Law School has long been a mentor on issues of constitutional criminal law; his intellect, along with his personal faith and courage, is inspirational.

My editor at *The Washington Post*, Fred Hiatt, permitted me the time off I needed to complete this project. I spent two months' leave as a Bosch Public Policy Fellow at the American Academy in Berlin, which proved the perfect environment to write, to reflect, and to absorb European perspectives on capital punishment in the United States. I am eternally grateful to Gary Smith, the Academy's effervescent executive director, for this wonderful opportunity; a thousand thanks also to Gary's staff—especially Christina Woelpert, Ulrike Graalfs, and Yolande Korb—who did so much to ensure that my family and I had everything we needed for a successful stay.

During the writing of this book, my family has been my greatest source of strength and happiness, as they always are. To my children, David, Nina, and Johanna, thanks for your energy, curiosity, patience, and love; and to my wife, Cati, thanks once again, for everything.

Charles Lane
Washington, D.C.

August 2009

ENDNOTES

Preface

1. Confidential author interview with Texas state official, January 2009.
2. Death Penalty Information Center, "Executions in the U.S., 1608-2002: The Espy File," http://deathpenaltyinfo.org/executions-us-1608-2002-espy-file (accessed May 3, 2009); "The Death Penalty in 2008: Year End Report, December 2008," http://www.deathpenaltyinfo.org/2008YearEnd.pdf (accessed May 3, 2009).
3. U.S. Department of Justice, Bureau of Justice Statistics, "Capital Punishment Statis-

tics," http://www.ojp.usdoj.gov/bjs/cp. htm (accessed May 4, 2009).

4. Death Penalty Information Center, "The Death Penalty in 2008."

One

1. Unless otherwise noted, all public opinion data regarding capital punishment in this book are from a summary document on The Gallup Poll's official Website, "Death Penalty," http://www.gallup.com/poll/1606/Death-Penalty.aspx (accessed March 23, 2009).

2. Stuart Banner, *The Death Penalty: An American History*, (Cambridge Mass.: Harvard University Press, 2002), p. 244.

3. Margaret Werner Callahan, *Historical Corrections Statistics in the United States, 1850–1984* (Rockville, Md.: U.S. Department of Justice, 1986), pp. 18–19.

4. Banner, *The Death Penalty*, pp. 246–47.

5. For a compilation of materials on the Illi-

nois cases, see Death Penalty Information Center, "Illinois Commission on Capital Punishment," http://www.deathpenalty-info.org/node/674 (accessed August 29, 2009).

6. John Futty, "Death-penalty cases in Franklin County becoming rarer," *Columbus Dispatch*, November 3, 2008, p. 1A.

7. Andrew Welsh-Huggins, "Ohio prosecutors using new life without parole option," Associated Press, June 22, 2008.

8. For an example of how an Ohio death-row inmate, Clifton White, won a reduction in his death sentence to life without parole by convincing a court he was mentally retarded, see Bob Driehaus, "Death Sentence is Overturned in Ohio," *The New York Times*, April 10, 2008, p. 21.

9. *Atkins v. Virginia*, 536 U.S. 304 (2002); *Roper v. Simmons*, 543 U.S. 551 (2005). In 1989, the court had upheld capital punishment for a moderately retarded Texas offender (*Penry v. Lynaugh*, 492 U.S. 302) and for a 16-year-old Kentuckian (*Stanford v. Kentucky*, 492 U.S. 361).

10. *Ring v. Arizona* 536 U.S. 584 (2002).

11. *Baze v. Rees* 553 U.S. 35 (2008).

12. Data for all Gallup Polls since 1936 are found at The Gallup Poll's official Website,

"Death Penalty," http://www.gallup.com/poll/1606/Death-Penalty.aspx (accessed March 23, 2009).

13. *Callins v. Collins*, 510 U.S. 1141, 1130 (1994) (Blackmun, J., dissenting from denial of certiorari).

14. Lydia Saad, "Americans Hold Firm to Support for Death Penalty," Gallup News Service, November 17, 2008, http://www.gallup.com/poll/111931/americans-hold-firm-support-death-penalty.aspx (Accessed March 23, 2009); Jeffrey M. Jones, "Support for the Death Penalty 30 Years After the Supreme Court Ruling: Two in three currently support it," Gallup News Service, June 30, 2006, http://www.gallup.com/poll/23548/Support-Death-Penalty-Years-After-Supreme-Court-Ruling.aspx (accessed March 23, 2009).

15. Quinnipiac University, "American Voters Oppose Same-Sex Marriage Quinnipiac University, National Poll Finds, But They Don't Want Government To Ban It," July 17, 2008, http://www.quinnipiac.edu/x1295.xml?ReleaseID=1194 (accessed May 20, 2009).

16. Associated Press, AP-Ipsos International Poll, "Attitudes Toward the Death Penalty," April 26, 2007, http://hosted.ap.org/spe-

cials/interactives/wdc/int_deathpenalty/i ndex.html (accessed May 18, 2009); ibid.

17. John Blume, Theodore Eisenberg, and Martin T. Wells, "Explaining Death Row's Population and Racial Composition," *Journal of Empirical Legal Studies*, vol. 1, no. 1 (March 2004), pp. 180, 205.

18. Death Penalty Information Center, "Legislative Activity—Wisconsin," http://www. deathpenaltyinfo.org/legislative-activity-wisconsin (accessed May1, 2009).

19. Charles Lane, "Court Bars Execution of Mentally Retarded," *The Washington Post*, June 21, 2002, p. A1.

20. Charles Lane, "5-4 Supreme Court Abolishes Juvenile Executions," *The Washington Post*, March 2, 2005, p. A1.

21. Samuel R. Gross and Pheobe Ellsworth, "Second Thoughts: Americans' Views on the Death Penalty at the Turn of the Century," in Stephen P. Garvey, ed., *Beyond Repair? America's Death Penalty* (Durham, N.C.: Duke University Press, 2003), p. 16.

22. Banner, *The Death Penalty*, p. 223.

23. U.S. Department of Justice, Bureau of Justice Statistics (derived from "Vital Statistics of the United States, National Center for Health Statistics"), http://www.ojp.gov/bjs/glance /sheets/hmrt.csv (accessed April 15, 2009).

24. U.S. Department of Justice, Bureau of Justice Statistics, "Capital Punishment Statistics," http://www.ojp.usdoj.gov/bjs/cp.htm (accessed May 20, 2009).

25. U.S. Department of Justice, Bureau of Justice Statistics (derived from "Vital Statistics of the United States, National Center for Health Statistics"), http://www.ojp.gov/bjs/glance/sheets/hmrt.csv (accessed April 15, 2009).

26. U.S. Department of Justice, Homicide trends in the U.S., "Homicide victimization, 1950–2005," http://www.ojp.usdoj.gov/bjs/homicide/tables/totalstab.htm (accessed April 15, 2009).

27. Ibid., and subsequent annual reports on homicide contained in FBI Uniform Crime Reports.

28. *Ewing v. California*, 538 U.S. 11 (2003); *Lockyer v. Andrade*, 538 U.S. 63 (2003).

29. Blume, Eisenberg, and Wells, "Explaining Death Row's Population," p. 187.

30 Ibid., pp. 172, 187.

31. *Furman v. Georgia*, 408 U.S. 238, 309 (1972).

32. Banner, *The Death Penalty*, p. 268.

33. *Gregg v. Georgia*, 428 U.S. 153, 179 (1976) (joint opinion of Stewart, Powell, and Stevens, JJ.).

34. Herbert Haines, quoted in Jeffrey L. Kirchmeier, "Another Place Beyond Here: The
Death Penalty Moratorium Movement in
the United States," *University of Colorado
Law Review*, vol. 73, no. 1 (2002), p. 75.
Much of the history in this chapter is derived from Kirchmeier's article, as well as
from Banner, *The Death Penalty*, pp. 208–
306.

Two

1. George F. Will, "Innocent on Death Row," *The Washington Post*, April 6, 2000, p. A23.
2. Table 6.86, "Prisoners executed under civil authority by race and offense, 1930-1998," *Sourcebook of Criminal Justice Statistics 2003*, http://www.albany.edu/source-book/pdf/t686.pdf (accessed May 22, 2009).
3. Ibid.
4. Banner, *The Death Penalty*, p. 255.
5. Ibid., p. 265.
6. *Gregg*, 428 U.S. 153, 189 (1976) (joint opinion of Stewart, Powell, and Stevens, JJ.).
7. *Coker v. Georgia*, 433 U.S. 584 (1977).
8. Death Penalty Information Center, "Race of Death Row Inmates Executed Since 1976," http://www.deathpenaltyinfo.org/race-

death-row-inmates-executed-1976 (accessed December 30, 2008); Table 6.80.2009, "Prisoners Under Sentence of Death, by Race, Ethnicity, and Jurisdiction, on Jan. 1, 2009," Sourcebook of Criminal Justice Statistics Online, http://www.albany.edu/sourcebook/pdf/t 6802009.pdf (accessed August 31, 2009).

9. Linda E. Carter and Ellen Kreitzberg, *Understanding Capital Punishment Law* (Newark, N.J.: Lexis-Nexis, 2004), pp. 292–93.

10. *McCleskey v. Kemp*, 481 U.S. 279, 293, 298 fn. 20 (1987).

11. John Calvin Jeffries, *Justice Lewis F. Powell, Jr.* (New York: Charles Scribners Sons, 1994), p. 415. After his retirement from the court, Powell also expressed his support for abolition of capital punishment. Ibid.

12. Blume, Eisenberg, and Wells, "Explaining Death Row's Population," pp. 189-90.

13. Ibid., pp. 166, 189.

14. Ibid., pp. 190, 192.

15. Violence Policy Center, "Black Homicide Victimization in the United States: An Analysis of 2006 Data," Washington D.C., January 2009, p. 2.

16. Blume, Eisenberg, and Wells, "Explaining Death Row's Population," p. 192.

17. In a 2007 survey, Gallup reported that 56 percent of blacks opposed the death penalty for murder, whereas only 26 percent of whites opposed it. Lydia Saad, "Racial Disagreement Over Death Penalty Has Varied Historically," Gallup News Service, July 30, 2007, http://www.gallup.com /poll/28243/racial-disagreement-over-death-penalty-has-varied-historically.aspx (accessed March 23, 2009).

18. Theodore Eisenberg, "Death Sentence Rates and County Demographics: An Empirical Study," *Cornell Law Review*, vol. 90, no. 2 (January, 2005), p. 370.

19. Maryland Department of Public Safety and Corrections, "Maryland's Death Penalty: A Synopsis," http://dpscs.maryland.gov/ publicinfo/capitalpunishment/synopsis.s html (accessed June 4, 2009); John Roman, et al. "The Cost of the Death Penalty in Maryland," Urban Institute Justice Policy Center Research Report, March 2008, p. 1; Maryland Citizens Against Executions, "Maryland's Death Row," http://www.mdcase.org/node/24 (accessed June 4, 2009).

20. Lori Montgomery, "The Wrong Place to Commit a Murder," *The Washington Post*, May 12, 2002, p. C7.

21. Percel Odel Alston Jr., et al., Maryland Commission on Capital Punishment: Final Report to the General Assembly (Minority Report), December 12, 2008, p. 12, http://www.goccp.maryland.gov/capital-punishment/documents/death-penalty-commission-final-report.pdf (accessed May 6, 2009).

22. Michael Ponsor, "Life, Death, and Uncertainty," *The Boston Globe*, July 8, 2001, p. D2.

23. Michael L. Radelet, "The Role of the Innocence Argument in Contemporary Death Penalty Debates," *Texas Tech Law Review*, vol. 41, no. 1 (Fall 2008), p. 219.

24. *United States v. Quinones*, 205 F. Supp. 2d 256, 257 (S.D.N.Y. 2002). Judge Rakoff's ruling was subsequently reversed by the New York-based United States Court of Appeals for the Second Circuit. *United States v. Quinones*, 313 F.3d 49 (2d Cir. 2002).

25. *Kansas v. Marsh*, 548 U.S. 163, 210 (2006) (Souter, J., dissenting).

26. Ibid., pp. 188, 193, 199 (Scalia, J., concurring).

27. Editorial, "Death Row and DNA," *The Washington Post*, December 16, 2000, p. A26.

28. See Death Penalty Information Center, "The Innocence List," http://www.deathpenalty-

info.org/innocence-list-those-freed-death-row (accessed April 9, 2009).

29. Maria Glod and Michael Shear, "DNA Tests Confirm Guilt of Executed Man," *The Washington Post*, January 13, 2006, p. A1.

30. Ibid.

31. Brooke A. Masters, "High Profile Case Ends in Va. Execution," *The Washington Post*, September 15, 2000, p. B1.

32. Joshua Rozenberg, "DNA proves Hanratty guilt 'beyond doubt'," *Daily Telegraph*, May 11, 2002, p. 10.

33. See Charles Lane, "Disorder in the Court," *The Washington Post*, November 12, 2001, p. A3; Alan Johnson, "Inmate's claim of innocence is denied," *The Columbus Dispatch*, November 30, 2001, p. 1C.

34. Death Penalty Information Center, "The Innocence List."

35. Ibid.; Ward A. Campbell, "Critique of DPIC List," paper presented at 2002 annual conference of the Association of Government Attorneys in Capital Litigation, http://www.prodeathpenalty.com/DPIC.htm (accessed April 6, 2009); Matthew Walberg, "Judge's injustice is righted—23 years later," *Chicago Tribune*, April 9, 2009, p. 1; Rumanna Hussain, "Ex-gang 'general' goes from Death Row to not guilty," *Chicago Sun-*

Times, April 8, 2009, p. 10. See also Ward A. Campbell, "Exoneration Inflation: Justice Scalia's Concurrence in *Kansas v. Marsh*," *IACJ Journal*, Summer 2008, pp. 49–61.

36. Campbell, "Exoneration Inflation," p. 55; *In re Jones*, 13 Cal.4th 552 (1996); Rebecca Taylor, "Murder Convict Walking: Merced Case Too Old to Retry, DA Grouses," *The Modesto Bee*, November 16, 1996, p. A1.

37. Ibid.; Ramesh Ponnuru, "Bad List," *National Review*, September 16, 2002; *Marsh*, 548 U.S. 163, 196 (Scalia, J., concurring); Joseph Morton and Leslie Reed, "Sheets Set Free," *Omaha World-Herald*, June 13, 2001, p. 1.

38. *Quinones*, 205 F. Supp. 2d 256, 265, n. 11.

39. Author analysis of cases on DPIC List. See also Campbell, "Exoneration Inflation," pp. 61–62.

40. Author analysis of cases on DPIC List.

41. Campbell, "Critique."

Three

1. John Dewey, *The Essential Dewey: Pragmatism, Education, Democracy*, Larry A. Hickman and Thomas M. Alexander, eds. (Bloomington, Ind.: Indiana University Press, 1998), p. 294.
2. 489 U.S. 288 (1989).
3. Anita Kumar, "Kaine Vetoes Bills to Expand Death Penalty," *The Washington Post*, March 28, 2009, p. B3.
4. Campbell, "Critique."
5. Cass Sunstein and Adrian Vermuele, "Is Capital Punishment Morally Required? Acts, Omissions, and Life-Life Tradeoffs," *Stanford Law Review*, vol. 58, no. 3 (December, 2005), p. 703.
6. Quoted in Jeff Jacoby, "The cost of a death-penalty moratorium," *Jewish World Review*,

June 7, 2002, http://www.jewishworl-dreview.com/jeff/jacoby060702.asp (accessed May 2, 2009).

7. John J. Donohue and Justin Wolfers, "Uses and Abuses of Empirical Evidence in the Death Penalty Debate," *Stanford Law Review*, vol. 58, no. 3 (December, 2005), p. 791.

8. Ibid., p. 843.

9. *Baze v. Rees*, 553 U. S. 35 (2008) (Stevens, J., concurring) (slip op., at 10).

10. "Andrew Welsh-Huggins, The Associated Press, "Analysis Shows Death Sentences Imposed Inconsistently in Ohio," *Akron Beacon-Journal*, May 7, 2005," p. A1.

11. Texas Department of Criminal Justice, "Total Number of Offenders Sentenced to Death from Each County," http://www.tdcj.state.tx.us/stat/county-sentenced.htm (accessed April 14, 2009).

12. Washington State Department of Corrections, "Offenders Currently Under Sentence of Death," http://www.doc.wa.gov/offenderinfo/capitalpunishment/sentencedlist.asp (accessed April 15, 2009).

13. Matthew R. Wilmot, "Sparing Gary Ridgway: The Demise of the Death Penalty in Washington State?" *Willamette Law Review*, vol. 41, no. 2 (Spring 2005), p. 435.

14. Eisenberg, "Death Sentence Rates and County Demographics," p. 349.

15. Quoted in Adam Liptak, "Study Revises Texas' Standing as a Death Penalty Leader," *The New York Times*, February 14, 2004, p. 10.

16. Benjamin R. Civiletti, et al., Maryland Commission on Capital Punishment: Final Report to the General Assembly, December 12, 2008, p. 11, http://www.goccp.maryland.gov/capital-punishment/documents/death-penalty-commission-final-report.pdf (accessed May 6, 2009).

17. Matthew Preusch, "Families Speak as Green River Killer Gets 48 Life Terms," *The New York Times*, December 19, 2003, p. 24.

18. Alston Jr., et al., Maryland Commission on Capital Punishment, p. 11.

19. Kate Roberts, "Capital Cases Put Squeeze on Smaller Counties," Associated Press State & Local Wire, May 3, 2005.

20. Table 6.0002.2005, "Prisoners under sentence of death and outcome of the sentence, United States, by year of sentencing 1973-2005," Sourcebook of Criminal Justice Statistics Online, http://www.albany.edu/sourcebook/pdf/t600022005.pdf (accessed May 13, 2009); Death Penalty Information Center, Year-End Reports for

2006-2008; Ibid., "Executions in the United States by State," http://www.deathpenaltyinfo.org/executions-united-states-1608-1976-state (accessed May 3, 2009); Ibid., "Death Sentences in the United States From 1977 to 2007," http://www.deathpenaltyinfo.org/death-sentences-united-states-1977-2007 (accessed May 4, 2009).

21. Ibid.

22. Gerald Uelmen, ed., California Commission on the Fair Administration of Justice, Final Report, June 30, 2008, p. 124.

23. Franklin E. Zimring, *The Contradictions of American Capital Punishment* (New York: Oxford University Press, 2003), pp. 89–118.

24. John R. Ross, "Lynching," Handbook of Texas Online," http://www.tshaonline.org/handbook/online/articles/LL/jgl1.html (accessed May 10, 2009).

25. Virginians for Alternatives to the Death Penalty, "Virginia Death Penalty Information," http://www.vadp.org/virginia-death-penalty-facts.html (accessed May 11, 2009).

26. Table 6.85.2008, "Prisoners executed under civil authority, by region and jurisdiction, 1930–2008," Sourcebook of Criminal Justice Statistics Online, http://

www.albany.edu/sourcebook/pdf/t685200 8.pdf (accessed May 28, 2009).

27. "Lynching by State and Race, 1882–1962," http://www.nathanielturner.com/lynchingbystateandrace.htm (accessed May 28, 2009).

28 Blume, Eisenberg, and Wells, "Explaining Death Row's Population," p. 172.

29. Frank Green, "Is evidence law for Va. felons too tough?" *Richmond Times-Dispatch*, July 16, 2007, p. A1. See also Joint Legislative Audit and Review Commission of the Virginia General Assembly, "Review of Virginia's System of Capital Punishment: Staff Briefing," December 10, 2001, http://jlarc.state.va.us/meetings/December01/capital.pdf (accessed May 3, 2009).

30. James Liebman, et al., "A Broken System: Error Rates in Capital Cases, 1973–1995," Columbia University research paper, June 12, 2000, http://www2.law.columbia.edu/instructionalservices/liebman/liebman_final.pdf (accessed April 30, 2009), p. 57.

31. See Texas Code of Criminal Procedure, Art. 11.071.

32. Nancy J. King, Fred L. Cheesman II, and Brian J. Ostrom, "Final Technical Report: Habeas Litigation in U.S. District Courts: An Empirical Study of Habeas Corpus

Cases Filed by State Prisoners Under the Antiterrorism and Effective Death Penalty Act of 1996," August 21, 2007, www.ncjrs.gov/pdffiles1/nij/grants/219558.pdf (accessed April 10, 2009), p. 21.

33. James Liebman, et al., "A Broken System, Part II: Why There Is So Much Error in Capital Cases, and What Can Be Done About It," Columbia University research paper, February 11, 2002, p. 334.

34. Uelmen, California Commission, p. 120, fn 21.

35. Dan Morain and Daniel M. Weintraub, "Wilson Rejects Plea of Mercy for Harris," *Los Angeles Times*, April 17, 1992, p. A1.

36. Katherine Bishop, "After Long Night of Legal Battles, California Carries Out Execution," *The New York Times*, April 22, 1992, p. A1; John T. Noonan, "Should State Executions Run on Schedule?" *The New York Times*, April 27, 1992, p. A17; California Department of Corrections and Rehabilitation, Reports & Research, "Robert Alton Harris," http://www.cdcr.ca.gov/Reports_Research/robertHarris.html (accessed April 2, 2009).

37. Uelmen, California Commission, p. 136; King, Cheesman, and Ostrom, "Final Technical Report," p. 32.

38. Uelmen, California Commission, pp. 136–37.
39. King, Cheesman, and Ostrom, pp. 32, 42.
40. *Commonwealth v. Steele*, 961 A.2d 786,837–38 (Pa. 2008) (Castille, J., concurring, with McCaffery, J.).
41. King, Cheesman, and Ostrom, p. 51.

Four

1. Civiletti, et al., Maryland Commission on Capital Punishment, p. 11.
2. John Wagner, "Md. Lawmakers Approve Tighter Death Penalty Rules," *The Washington Post*, March 26, 2009, p. B1.
3. Immanuel Kant, *Groundwork of the Metaphysics of Morals*, ed. Mary Gregor (Cambridge, Eng.: Cambridge University Press, 1996), p. 106.
4. Charles Lane, "On Death Row in Japan," *Policy Review*, no. 132, August-September 2005, http://www.hoover.org/publications/policyreview/2931521.html (accessed March 31, 2009); Paul Wiseman and Naoko Nishiwaki, "Japan Homicides Fall but Hangings Rise," *USA Today*, December 23, 2008, http://www.usatoday.com/

news/world/2008-12-23-japan-execution_n.htm (accessed March 30, 2009).

5. Quoted in *Asahi Weekly*, May 5, 2008 (see http://www.japanprobe.com/?p=4571).

6. Report of the Secretary-General of the United Nations Pursuant to Paragraph 2 of Security Council, Resolution 808 (1993), presented May 3, 1993, (S/25704) (Statute of the Tribunal), http://www.icty.org/x/file/Legal%20Library/Statute/statute_re808_1993_en.pdf (accessed May 20, 2009); Rome Statute of the International Criminal Court, Article 110, http://www2.icc-cpi.int/NR/rdonlyres/EA9AEFF7-5752-4F84-BE94-0A655EB30E16/0/Rome_Statute_English.pdf (accessed May 20, 2009).

7. Doreen Carvajal, "Saddam's Death Sentence Exposes a Rift," *International Herald Tribune*, December 28, 2006, http://www.nytimes.com/2006/12/28/world/africa/28iht-death.4042654.html (accessed April 10, 2009); Jeff Jacoby, "But more relief than regret," *The Boston Globe*, January 3, 2007, p. A11.

8. Allensbacher Institut, *Jahrbuch der Demoskopie, 1998-2002* (Munich: Verlag fuer Demoskopie, 2002), p. 676.

9. Daniel H. Foote, "The Door That Never

Opens?" Capital Punishment and Postconviction Review of Death Sentences in the United States and Japan," *Brooklyn Journal of International Law*, vol. 19 (1993), p. 383.

10. Author analysis of data presented in Jeffrey Kirchmeier, "Aggravating and Mitigating Factors: The Paradox of Today's Arbitrary and Mandatory Capital Punishment Scheme," *William & Mary Bill of Rights Journal*, vol. 6, no. 2 (Spring 1998); Jeffrey Kirchmeier, "Casting a Wider Net: Another Decade of Legislative Expansion of the Death Penalty in the United States," *Pepperdine Law Review*, vol. 34 (2006).

11. Uelmen, California Commission, pp. 120, 139.

12. Scott Phillips, "Racial Disparities in the Capital of Capital Punishment," *Houston Law Review*, vol. 45, no. 3 (Fall 2008), p. 833.

13. Montgomery; State of Illinois, *Report of the Governor's Commission on Capital Punishment*, April 15, 2002, p. 81. As this book went to press, a University of Houston law professor published a comprehensive proposal for such a state-wide system. See Adam M. Gershowitz, "Statewide Capital Punishment: The Case for Eliminating Counties' Role in the Death Penalty," forth-

coming in the *Vanderbilt Law Review*, vol. 62 (2010), http://papers.ssrn.com/sol3/papers.cfm?abstract_id=1457715 (accessed September 7, 2009).

14. Tracy Johnson, "Death Sentence Affirmed: Court Rules Inmate Can be Executed Despite Life for Ridgway," *Seattle Post-Intelligencer*, March 31, 2006, p. 1.

15. *Pulley v. Harris*, 465 U.S. 37 (1984).

16. See Timothy V. Kaufman-Osborn, "Proportionality Review and the Death Penalty," *The Justice System Journal*, vol. 29, no. 3 (2008).

17. Ibid., p. 259.

18. Kevin Johnson, "Prisoners' death row time doubles," *USA Today*, July 24, 2008, p. 1A.

19. Alex Kozinski and Sean Gallagher, "For an Honest Death Penalty," *The New York Times*, March 8, 1995, p. A15.

20. Rone Tempest, "Death Row Often Means a Long Life," *Los Angeles Times*, March 6, 2005, p. B1.

21. Kozinski and Gallagher, "For an Honest Death Penalty."

22. *Kennedy v. Louisiana*, 554 U.S. ___ (2008) (Alito, J., dissenting) (slip op., at 2).

23. Linda Greenhouse, "In Court Ruling on Executions, a Factual Flaw," *The New York Times*, July 2, 2008, p. A1; David G. Sav-

age, "Justices uphold death penalty ban in rape of a child," *Los Angeles Times*, October 2, 2008, p. 8.

INDEX